Copyright © Sanders Muleya

The moral rights of the author have been asserted.

All rights reserved. No part of this book may be reproduced, stored in a retrieval system, communicated or transmitted in any form or by any means without prior written permission.

All enquiries should be made to the author.

The 10x Property System - How To Amass 10 Properties in 10 Years And Retire Sooner

ISBN: 978-0-6452596-0-5

Disclaimer

The material in this publication is of the nature of general comment only, and does not represent professional advice. It is not intended to provide specific guidance for particular circumstances and it should not be relied on as the basis for any decision to take action or not take action on any matter which it covers.

Readers should obtain professional advice where appropriate, before making any such decision.

To the maximum extent permitted by law, the author and publisher disclaim all responsibility and liability to any person, arising directly or indirectly from any person taking or not taking action based on the information in this publication.

The 10x Property System

How To Amass 10 Properties in 10 Years And Retire Sooner

Sanders Muleya

Table of Contents

Dedication 1

Foreword 2

Chapter 1 - Sanders' Story – From an Immigrant Nurse to Achieving Financial Freedom Through Property in Under 10 Years 7

    My First Property..8

Chapter 2 - Why Property?..13

    Single Mum of Three Turn Property Investor 13

    Constant Growth Over 25 Years – The Story of the Australian Property Market 14

    Why Property Is the Asset of Choice for Australian Investors.....16

    Post-COVID – The Recovery Has Already Started 17

    Gearing for Super-Successful Property Investments....................19

Chapter 3 - Good Debt vs Bad Debt...20

    Leveraging 101 – What Is It and What Does It Mean? 21

    Good vs Bad Debt (and Why the Debt You Leverage for Property Is the Good Kind)..22

    What is the No. 1 Question for Property Investors?.....................24

    How to Use Leverage in Property Investment..............................25

    In Leverage We Trust 28

Chapter 4 - The Different Stages in Your Property Investment Journey...29

    Stage #1 – Accumulation..30

    Stage #2 – Consolidation 31

    Stage #3 – Generating Passive Income...33

    Stage #4 – Creating Legacy 34

    What's Your Stage?..35

**Chapter 5 - Getting Your First Property
(and the Crippling Mistakes Most People Make)**..................36

    Almost $300K in Profit in 12 Months............................36

    Getting Prepared to Invest in Property –
    The Seven Steps to Take...37

    These Are the Six Mistakes New Investors Make
    (That You Must Avoid)..40

    Due Diligence – Why Is It Important to Get This
    Right Before You Spend Any Money............................42

    Get Ready for Property Shopping..................................43

Chapter 6 - How to Get Your First Investment Property......45

    Understanding the Market – What You Need to Look
    for When Investing in Property......................................46

    Choosing the Right Location...49

    Getting Your Property Loan – How to Prepare
    the Perfect Application..51

    Ready, Steady, Buy...52

Chapter 7 - Why Negative Gearing Is a Bad Investment Strategy........53

    What Is Negative Gearing and How Does It Work?......54

    The Four Reasons Why Negative Gearing Is a
    Bad Idea for a New Investor..55

    Is Negative Gearing Ever a Good Idea?........................57

    Gear Your Properties Properly......................................59

**Chapter 8 - How to Fast Track Your Investments
Using Property Professionals**...60

    Getting on the Right Track..61

    Get Your Long-Term Goals Straight.............................62

    How to Find the Right Buyer's Agent...........................63

    Benefits of Mortgage Brokers.......................................64

    Assemble Your Property Investment Team...................65

Chapter 9 - Property Types – Which One to Aim For 67
    The Types 68
    What Property Type Did You Choose? 72

Chapter 10 - Creative Strategies 74
    The Strategies 75
    Get Your Creative Juices Flowing 79

Chapter 11 - Using Equity to Grow Your Property Portfolio 81
    The Equity You Could Get From a Duplex 82
    In Equity We Trust 84

Chapter 12 - The Strategy – Ten Properties in Ten Years 86
    Getting the 10 Properties 87

Chapter 13 - Using Property as Your Retirement Vehicle 92
    Explaining the Australian Retirement Crisis 93
    Can Property Provide a Good Return for Retirement? 95
    Seven Property Techniques You Can Use to Make
    Property Your Retirement Vehicle 96
    Carefree Retirement 99

Chapter 14 - Positive Cash Flow is King –
How to Be Your Own Boss 101
    What Does Investing for Positive Cash Flow Mean? 102
    The Benefits of Investing in Positive Cash Flow 103
    Four Tips for Finding Positive Cash Flow Properties 105
    Focus on the Positive 107

Chapter 15 - Retire in Style – Investing Through
a Self-Managed Super Fund 108
    What Are SMSFs? 109
    How to Invest in Property Using an SMSF 110
    The Five Tips for Using an SMSF to Invest
    (and Ensure You Meet All Regulations) 112

Make a Super Comfortable Retirement 115

Chapter 16 - Mindset and Goal Setting 116

    The Six Mindset Habits That Set You Up for Investing Success 117

    Three Tips for Setting Realistic and Achievable Goals 121

    Getting the Right Mindset 122

Chapter 17 - Procrastination vs Action Taking 124

    The True Costs of Procrastination in Property 125

    Overcoming Your Fear to Take Action 127

    Turning Procrastination into Action – The Five Tips 130

    Don't Procrastinate 132

Chapter 18 - Your Future and Where You're Now 133

    Why Is Property a Good Choice? 134

    Getting Into Your Investor Journey 134

    Negative Gearing Revisited 135

    The Retirement of Your Dreams 136

    Get Into the Investor Mindset 136

Dedication

This book is dedicated to my family – my beautiful and supportive wife Sikhumbuzo, and our wonderful children: Musa, Sandra, and Steve. You inspire me each and every day.

I wouldn't have prospered and achieved these milestones without your wonderful companionship.

To my late father and mother, who nurtured me to be the type of person I am today despite their limited financial resources, you cannot be overlooked. Your inspiration lives on, and I will pass it on to generations to come. Your parental guidance has been second to none.

It is also dedicated to several mentors and coaches who have guided me throughout my business journey. Your encouragement towards me believing in myself and quitting a nursing job to pursue financial freedom through property investing is phenomenal. Your experience and advice have been invaluable.

You have massively helped me achieve my largest goals, and now I am helping others achieve the same. This is the only way I can give back to the community.

Finally, this is dedicated to my readers and clients. May you find property investment wisdom in these pages and nuggets to help guide you towards your own personal pathway to success.

If you take action, you will succeed. You are your own enemy of success.

Taking action breeds success. Procrastination leads to failure.

Change the way you do things, or nothing will change.

Foreword

The plan to write this book came to my mind in 2021, once I made up my mind to leave nursing and pursue my passion as a property investor and a business entrepreneur. I had given 33 years of my life saving lives, and this was the time to pivot and save my own and others' financial future through positive cash flow and instant equity property investing. I managed to raise my family, buy a home to live in, and put food on the table through nursing, until I reached the ceiling.

Each time I thought of how my retirement would look like through this means, I got super scared and had sleepless nights. How long would I work? When would I enjoy freedom? Be financially free? Be able to travel and spend time with my family? I wanted a life full of choices.

The idea of property investment started at a very young age, when I was 15, back in Zimbabwe where I built my own investment in Binga while transporting building materials from Hwange on a bus.

Once in Australia, I had made a lot of costly property investment mistakes, but I never gave up.

I educated myself on all types of property investment strategies through the support of my family and successful property mentors.

I then chose the positive cash flow strategy in conjunction with property developments, and the rest is history.

I have spent the past 15 years of my life in Australia buying and selling properties. My property investments have allowed me to build my wealth, ensuring that my family and myself continue to enjoy a comfortable lifestyle in the foreseeable future and beyond. I have built a secure future, which includes no fear for retirement, education for my children, and the ability to travel when and where I wish. I have built prosperity for my loved ones and can now follow our passion wherever they might lead us.

I have bought, sold, and developed properties worth millions of dollars. At first, I did this to build my own wealth, but soon, I began buying properties for my clients, helping them build their wealth through well-researched properties. Since then, through my company Msisa Property and Consulting, I have helped thousands of Australians build their wealth through positive cash flow properties and property developments.

Through my extensive property investment expertise, I have guided and helped create many of Australia's new property millionaires. For me, this is perhaps the most secure route to unlocking property wealth in the country we live in. I have tried other forms of investments, but I have found property investments to be the fastest and most secure way to turn a small amount of equity into the most rewarding, prosperous financial future.

Each time you apply the positive cash flow strategy, you will be growing your wealth, creating extra income for yourself, turning a small nest egg into a portfolio of income-generating and wealth-building assets without relying on your job.

The strategy works because it is the same strategy that I have used to become a property millionaire.

I was not born a millionaire; I had to work and earn it. My first job was working as a migrant nurse in hospitals, nursing homes, disability centres through most states of Australia. I had to endure cultural differences and work two to three jobs and long hours just to raise a family. I dreamt of wealth, freedom, and recognition, and I was taught that to get ahead, you had to work very hard. Each time I encountered difficulties, I would remember my father's advice that "success had to be planned for".

Have a vision, plan well, believe in yourself, and execute your newfound ideas – success will follow.

This made me constantly think of my future, and it wasn't long before I started investing in bricks and mortar. I knew it was tangible, predictable, secure; most importantly, if chosen carefully, it would make me never dependent on my employer forever, beyond retirement.

After making numerous mistakes that I corrected through education and self-belief, I found myself buying a property every year until I replaced my income. I knew what I needed to do, and I knew property was the only ladder to allow me to climb my way out of misery, poverty, and be able to quit my nursing job. Losing my job at Westmead Hospital as a nurse in 2008 during the Global Financial Crisis meant leaving my family for a year in Sydney while I travelled to Tasmania to work as a nurse.

It made me realise that anything can happen to you, even if you think you have a secure job.

You are only a number and can be replaced at any time, no matter how good an employee you are.

After the crisis in 2010, I came back home to Sydney and methodically started the property investment process, when everyone was still scared and recovering from the Global Financial Crisis.

Everyone around me screamed at me that it was the wrong time to invest and I would lose money again, but I have learnt that you need to be greedy when others are fearful and be fearful when others are greedy. The most successful businesses grew substantially into empires during the recession or difficult times, e.g., Microsoft, Disney and Apple; I did the same by buying a lot of properties at a reduced price. My plan was to one day get out of a 9-to-5 job, step by step but systematically. I was always dreaming of being my own boss and financially free.

Opportunity waits for nobody. And so, in 2019, I formed my business – Msisa Property and Consulting.

My business scaled up a year later during the COVID-19 pandemic, when others were super scared and tightening their belts. As a wise investor, I knew to both disregard mob fears and enthusiasm and to focus on a few simple, well-researched fundamentals. With solid fundamentals, Msisa Property and Consulting flourished as it was established as an inspired purpose to help others achieve phenomenal wealth the same way I did. The purpose – to help everyday Australians build and preserve wealth through positive cash flow property investments. During the COVID-19 pandemic in 2020, we helped a lot of our clients buy a lot of well-researched real estate using the same strategy of seizing the moment when there is fear.

There were plenty of properties on the market for sale, but there were very few buyers, which gave us buyers an upper hand to negotiate and buy below the market value. Fast track a year later – 2021, property values went up substantially like no other time before.

This is the twofold legacy I want to leave behind. I want my family to be prosperous and financially secure, and I also want to give back to the community and my country by helping people have a prosperous and meaningful future. We need to work smarter and not harder.

My dream has always been to leave a legacy of wealth and security for my family, but my other legacy will also be the wealth I have helped and continue to deliver for my clients.

This book will further my legacy by helping other people and readers build their wealth through positive cash flow property investments. This book is the key to prosperity and financial security right in your hands. Reading this inspirational book will change the way you think about the future ahead and how you can pivot and live your life to the fullest.

The only way I want to be remembered as a success, and a man who helped others become wealthy, is through this book. This is the way I believe I can change those around me and the country, or even the world. I want to change people's lives by reducing financial worries, especially around retirement, as it pains me to see people working until their 70s as they have no choice but to work until they are stopped by age or ill health. My aim is to alleviate all forms of debt for clients, including the escalating credit card debt, and make families secure, no matter what their situation is.

I want prosperity to flow from current to future generations, parents buying properties for their children and vice versa – all in the name of Msisa Property and Consulting.

The door has been opened, and all you need to do is enter and start adding properties to your portfolio, thereby opening multiple doors. This is the only way your financial insecurities and unanswered questions about your future can be addressed forever.

I made numerous investment mistakes, as I had no one to advise me or hold my hand.

I then made the right choices.

I am now financially free through property investing.

Take control of your financial future by making the right choices, the same way I did.

I left my nursing career purely to help others… you can be one of them.

The choice is yours.

The door is wide open.

All you need to do is walk through the door.

The coming pages will change your life for good.

Keep reading, and the sky's the limit.

CHAPTER 1

Sanders' Story – From an Immigrant Nurse to Achieving Financial Freedom Through Property in Under 10 Years

This book is a story about triumph. It's also a book about overcoming incredibly long odds to create a financially successful life. Finally, this is about a book that will guide you through the steps to creating financial freedom in property investing.

My name is Sanders, and my goal is simple…

I want to inspire you to invest in property and secure your financial future!

So, let's dig into my story.

I was born and grew up in the remote part of Binga, in the Matabeleland North province, Zimbabwe. My parents were peasant farmers and could hardly afford to raise enough money to send me to school. I used to travel a total of 30 kilometres to and from school bare footed. My parents could not afford to buy a school uniform, and could hardly afford to buy educational material.

To be able to afford to pay for my education, I had to work very hard in my parents' farm during the school holidays. I could then sell the produce like tomatoes, onions, bananas etc., and be able to pay for books, school fees as well as examination fees.

Despite these hardships I managed to pass my final examinations with good grades, and pursued nursing as a career. I never dreamt of leaving Zimbabwe until there was an economic downturn. I could see no bright future for me and my family, and therefore I made a decision to leave the country.

I applied for nursing Jobs in the UK and Australia, and was very lucky to get accepted in Australia.

To be able to pay for a working visa, register with the Australian nursing council, as well as raise air fares for myself and the entire family, I had to sell everything we owned, except my family.

Where there is a will there is always a way, and I had to do absolutely everything to leave the country so as to secure a better future in Australia.

Coming from a minority tribe in Zimbabwe, I have come a long way since arriving in Australia with my wife and three kids.

At the time, we only had $50 and had to learn everything about a new culture, people, and environment. Suffice to say, the differences between Australia and Zimbabwe are long and detailed! :) Plus, I didn't know anyone in Australia.

Now, my family had to make a life in the country. The silver lining was that I had a job waiting for me when we arrived. But living in Australia on a single salary is next to impossible, particularly when you have three children who need schooling and a roof over their heads.

I mean, we had to buy a family home to live in and raise our children. And that was extremely difficult given my background and the challenges of adapting to a culture that's worlds apart from my home country.

My wife and I had to work two jobs to make it all happen.

My First Property

By 2006 though, which is two years after I settled in Australia, I acquired my first permanent place of residence (PPR).

Remember, I landed in this incredible country with $50 in my pocket and the responsibility to support my wife and three kids. I was proud of myself and proud of my wife for supporting me.

But it doesn't end there.

I soon realised that property investment was my passion. And after acquiring my second property, I then tried to acquire my third.

But unfortunately, this is when I realised I made a fatal mistake.

I purchased the second property for about $100,000 over the market value – way, way above market! Not only that, but the rent was meagre, and I struggled to return what I invested. To be honest, I started haemorrhaging money and that affected my family as well. So, I tried to come up with some kind of exit strategy.

The obvious choice was to go to the bank to get additional funding for property number three. But the bank refused to finance the deal because I was overstretched, and the second property was cross collateralised with our home.

Some novice investors might've been discouraged by this refusal, but I wasn't!

I didn't give up and took a second job so I could start reinvesting. In 2010, I eventually got out of the mess I created and got really serious about investing.

Benefits of Having the Right Strategy

By this time, I tried my luck with renovations, house and land packages, off-the-plan purchases, etc. Unfortunately, I finally ran out of money and decided to change course.

Thankfully, by this time, I had a much better idea of what needed to get done.

I set my sights on developments because I wanted to make sure I could buy a property every year whenever I wanted. And I haven't looked back since because developments turned out to be the name of my game.

I'll get back to my investments later in this book. But there is a more important point you can take from my strategy for the moment.

Most of us rely heavily on our income to secure our retirement plans. But when retirement comes, it often turns out that there's not enough money to provide you with a decent lifestyle. However, there's a much better way to secure your retirement long before you come to retirement age!

Now, let me tease your imagination a little and tell you exactly how your property strategy may play out.

Imagine this, you buy a property for $400,000 when you're 25, and your mortgage will typically be for 30 years. By the time you're 55, you'll have paid off the property entirely, and it could be worth more than $1 million.

But, there's even a better way.

Since you want to start investing, you'd want to leverage the increase in value of the first property and buy another property every year or every two years. So, at the end of the 20-year period, you'll have more than ten properties with a valuation worth $10 million.

In retirement, this gives you a lot of choices. For example, you can sell off five and keep the remaining properties debt-free. Then, you can rent out the properties you possess and have a sizeable passive income every year for the rest of your life.

What a dream!

But I must admit, even though I had the dream, I didn't yet have the skill I needed to make it a reality.

That was my big realisation.

Early on, I understood I needed more education about all things relating to property investment. So, I dived headfirst into learning everything and anything I could about the Australian real estate market. I kept staying up late to read Australian financial reviews to understand all the nuances of the market.

I attended seminars, went to courses, and spent $100K on property education, I developed a peer group... I did everything and anything I could to become successful and wealthy and to support my three lovely kids and my beautiful wife.

And the result...

I'm happy to report that from 2010 to 2019, I acquired 15 properties in my portfolio. An even better news is that I never ever repeated the mistake of overpaying for a property, and I kept growing my portfolio. And most importantly, I replaced my income threefold through property and left my 9-to-5 job.

What a dream come true.

Scared of Investing?

Here's the thing...

There's nothing to fear when investing in properties. The Australian population is growing, and everybody needs a roof over their head! So, there will be no shortage of prospective buyers even if there are some intermissions in demand.

Then there's migration, of which there's a lot. I can tell you, Australia is a wonderful place to live. And all over the world, it's known as the Lucky Country. Migration is a powerful driving force behind rising property prices.

In other words, for investors, that's a good thing. Again, think about the potential...

When your first property increases in value, you have additional equity to invest in. With that equity, you can buy your second property... and then your third.

And so on.

Of course, you don't have to wait for 20 years or until your property doubles in value. You can start reinvesting as soon as there's enough equity in your first property to secure the down payment for the second one.

And that's what I help others do today.

I believe that you can achieve anything in life as long as you want it enough. That's why I've used my knowledge of acquiring properties to help others achieve the same thing!

Now, I'm helping other people have the same level of freedom and financial stability that I have!

Over the next few chapters, I'll also talk more about the deals I've secured – both for myself and my clients.

CHAPTER 2

Why Property?

In the first chapter, you learned about me and the strategy that allowed me to build a portfolio of 15 properties. But I'm hardly the only person we helped achieve fantastic success in real estate.

So, I would like to show you that it's possible to be a single parent on a single income and still make it.

Single Mum of Three Turn Property Investor

This client came from Newcastle and was looking for opportunities to invest and secure some passive income. We considered her options and decided to go with the strategy that wouldn't put too much strain on her cash flow.

So, we opted to go for a cash flow-positive property from the get-go.

We found a double-storey house with two bedrooms upstairs and one bedroom downstairs. These were all self-contained, so she could rent them separately.

Basically, she had two tenants and two rents in a single property. More importantly, the deal came with 895sqm of land, giving her the option to build another property in the future and increase both her cash flow and equity.

But the real beauty of this deal is evident when you look at the numbers.

The asking price before the purchase was $355,000, and we managed to negotiate it down to $340,000, saving the client $15,000 right at the start.

The two rentals within the property bring in $550 a week, and the total rental yield is 8.4%, turning a residential tenancy into a commercial rental return.

All in all, she got the best deal she could, but it's not only about the money she started making right away. The property has fantastic growth potential. Plus, there's room for construction on the land.

Constant Growth Over 25 Years – The Story of the Australian Property Market

According to the Aussie/CoreLogic report, the Australian property market has increased manifold between 1993 and 2018. Since the housing market was so strong, the median house value leapt by a staggering 412%.

Let's put this into context...

In 1993, the median value of a home was $123,840. Over the past 25 years, the annual growth rate was about 6.8% for homes.

And for units, it was 5.9%.

Translated into dollars, the typical home is now about $460,000 more expensive... and units' value jumped by $392,000.

Wow.

And this is only the beginning.

Look Forward to the Next 25 Years

Assuming that the given growth averages remain the same, there's a lot of room to accumulate a fortune in property.

I believe the trend is going to continue if not exceed the previous growth. After all, Australia is this beautiful land that offers plenty of opportunities for people like me and you.

The housing market will still follow its cycles. There will be periods of growth followed by a decline, but you can still expect a steady increase in value. From a historical perspective, the property cycles level out the growth volatility from one year to another.

For instance, long-term capital gains in Melbourne were the highest over the years. Nevertheless, the house values went through five different periods. Their values declined in specific years, only to spring back when the next growth cycle comes. Then, level out when they enter a cycle of stability.

But when you're considering property investments, home valuation isn't the only parameter to take into account.

On average, Australian mortgage sizes have followed the increase in property value. The annual increase rate was 6.4% a year. And the loan size was just shy of $400,000.

To stress, these are 2018 figures and they come from the Aussie/CoreLogic report. Currently, the numbers may look a bit different, but it doesn't mean the market stopped following its natural cycles.

Anyway, you should know that high-density living is also on the rise. Our client managed to get 895sqm of land, which was terrific. Stats show that available land for construction shrunk to 610sqm from 820sqm.

Also, Australian towns have changed their planning policies to allow for higher-density housing to compensate for the increase in population. Over the past few years, this kind of housing rose to 40% of all the construction and home sales.

But high-density housing in the cities isn't the only area that's likely to grow further.

Properties in the suburbs have also been on the rise, particularly in Melbourne, Sydney, Tasmania, and Perth. This trend has been exacerbated by the COVID-19 pandemic as more and more people are looking to escape the cities. Plus, they need a bigger space to allow them to efficiently work from home.

Indeed, the future of the Australian property market is promising. But potential growth is hardly the only reason you'd want to invest.

Why Property Is the Asset of Choice for Australian Investors

To give you a clear idea of why this asset class is the top choice, here's why property investment is so lucrative.

#1 – ROI (Return on Investment)

Rental yields provide a continuous ROI on the properties you own. At best, the returns will be higher compared to your mortgage, so the property will pay for itself. And if you're a first-time investor, we'd advise you to take advantage of this.

But there's also an option to get even higher returns. For example, the NDIS (National Disability Insurance Scheme) allows you to invest in SDA (Special Disability Accommodation). In doing so, you might be looking at an ROI of about 12%, which is much higher than average.

#2 – Tax Benefits

There are various tax benefits for property investors, depending on the type of property you get and your location. And you can even get tax benefits for negatively-geared properties on account of lost value from your property.

However, you shouldn't aim to invest in negatively-geared properties. This strategy requires experience and isn't recommended for first-time investors.

Other than that, ATO (Australian Tax Office) gives you the option to use a tax withholding variation. With this, you get a tax break every time you get a paycheque, and you don't need to wait for a year. Therefore, you can allocate these tax savings towards your property investments.

#3 – Abundance of Financing Options

Property mortgages are among the most popular products with different lenders. The great thing is that you shouldn't struggle to get your loan approved. Sure, this goes as long as your income isn't overstretched.

But you shouldn't worry too much about that because there are other financing options. Don't forget that I was overstretched and managed to create an amazing portfolio nonetheless.

Anyway, in addition to home loans, the lenders offer investment loans, primarily for commercial properties. And when you already have one property in your portfolio, getting the finance for the second one should be much easier.

But there's one thing to keep in mind.

The commercial property market has been slow in the past two years, primarily because of the pandemic. So, you should be extra cautious if you decide to invest there.

#4 – Security

In comparison to the stock market, for example, real estate is much more stable and offers lower risk. Additionally, the property market volatility gets reduced since it takes an extended period to liquidate a property. And it's not like unexpected disasters have significant long-term effects on the market.

Post-COVID – The Recovery Has Already Started

Experts predict that property prices will hit record highs in 2021.

Why?

There are different reasons that mostly boil down to a mix of the following:

- Very low interest rates
- Post-COVID lifestyle
- Government stimuli to beat recession

If you consider the current situation in Sydney, it's not hard to understand that average housing prices have already hit a record high. This coincides with the fact that most people living in the city started to look for their dream home in the outer regions.

In 2020, real estate agents in the Sydney area reported a double-digit increase in home valuations. The reason was that the supply of homes was limited, and there were a bunch of those who wanted to be closer to the beach.

For instance, Sydney residents began moving to the Northern Beaches because they didn't need to think about commuting to work. And it wasn't long before there were only a handful of homes available in the given area, driving the prices sky-high.

What's the Situation in Other Cities?

Across the board, major metropolitan areas in Australia are experiencing the same growth trend. In Melbourne, the capital growth in 2021 is expected to be between 8% and 12%. But Melbourne is hardly the only city with such exceptional potential.

Maybe unexpectedly, but the most significant increases happened in areas that were affected by COVID the most. Take Kwinana, which rose 8.7%, and Adelaide's Burnside is close behind at a 7.0% increase.

Also, you should consider the bigger picture to truly understand how and where the markets are going to move.

Under the assumption that we're going to keep COVID under control, real estate prices will hit a new record high by the end of the year.

To give you an idea of the kind of increase expected, we'll use the Sydney example again. Compared to pre-pandemic figures, the average house price in Sydney was up by $50,000. This happened in 2020 and set a new median price at about $1.22 million. In percentage, the increase was around 5.

But venture out to the suburbs and you'll realise the Northern Beaches experienced 10% growth only in the last year. This sounds great, but the Central Coast can be considered as the overall winner with close to a 13% increase.

With this in mind, it's important to stress that it's not always sunshine and roses in the property markets.

Inner-city property owners in Melbourne may expect negative equity, particularly for properties purchased prior to the pandemic. However, Melbourne's Mornington Peninsula and Maribyrnong appear unaffected, growing by 3.4% and 1.8%, respectively.

The reason for that could be partly due to the changing demographics of the investors.

Unlike before, it appears that upgraders and first-time buyers are driving the market forward. Also, the stock of lovely homes is in short supply. The moment something decent gets listed, it's immediately snapped up, often for a much higher price.

Gearing for Super-Successful Property Investments

When all is said and done, statistics and market changes don't lie. There's a lot of potential in the property market, particularly housing in the suburbs.

We want you to understand that growth won't stop. Okay, there could be brief intermissions and declines, but this doesn't thwart the long-term potential of your investment.

It's vital that you collect all the necessary information to know where and how much to invest. And if a property gives you the option to do construction down the line, don't think twice about snatching it from the market.

Even so, there are novice investors who are not sure how to get funding. This chapter touched upon debt and mortgages. But this topic is quite complex, so we've dedicated the next chapter to good and bad debt.

CHAPTER 3

Good Debt vs Bad Debt

This particular client of mine is an experienced investor and real estate developer. When we first met, he was searching for a townhouse development site.

The goal was to develop the property, of course. But first, the client wanted to hold it for a while with a rental return as he completed a few other projects.

That was an excellent strategy because it helped the client ensure no money was lost while waiting for due diligence, approvals, and funding. Simply put, the property had to provide immediate returns before it got developed.

But what kind of property did we find for this client?

The location was in Newcastle, NSW, and the size of the plot was 2,400sqm. There were two existing houses that provided dual rental income before demolition. And it gets even better.

The property was zoned R2 with the potential to build eight townhouses!

So let's talk numbers.

The initial asking price for the land and the two houses was $1.05 million. After some negotiations, we managed to drive the price down to $1.01 million, saving the client $40,000 right from the start.

Before development, the combined rental income on the two houses was $900 per week or $3,600 per month. The rental return was 4.45%, with a strong growth potential after taking advantage of the R2 zoning.

Now, the story of this client might sound a bit far-fetched for you. After all, this was an experienced investor with $1.05 million to play around with.

But I want you to think about his strategy carefully.

This client knew how to leverage his position and take full advantage of the characteristics that particular real estate provided.

There's no reason you can't do the same and get similar immediate returns, even with a much smaller investment.

To help you understand how to do that, I dedicated this chapter to leverage and debt.

Leveraging 101 – What Is It and What Does It Mean?

Without a doubt, there are numerous benefits to property investments.

For one, you can secure a stable recurring income and, over the years, you get excellent capital growth. Then, the risk of investing in properties is relatively low. And if you get burnt, like I did when I was starting out, it's not that hard to rebound.

Also, real estate investments are tax-efficient, but their most significant asset is the outstanding leverage potential.

What do I mean by that?

In the investment world, leveraging means you're borrowing funds to get an investment off the ground. Understandably, novice investors are hesitant to do that because they perceive borrowing as increasing the risk.

But take a moment to understand what you're getting by borrowing money.

When you leverage, you gain the upper hand to buy more real estate than you can currently afford to pay in full. In turn, you're growing your property investment portfolio and boosting the potential returns.

Sounds promising, right?

Even so, it's best to use a simple example to show you how leveraging works in a real-world scenario.

Say you have $50,000 to invest, you could deposit the money in a bank and earn a yearly interest of 3%. That amounts to $1,500 per year with no hassle and low risk.

Now, get into your property investor shoes and look at that money again.

A $50,000 deposit is enough for a $500,000 property. Let's assume a reasonable value increase of 3% per year, so you'll be earning $15,000, not a meagre $1,500.

Then, it pays to calculate the earnings from long-term capital growth in relation to that property value. I'd set a conservative capital growth of 8% a year. How much richer would that make you at the end of the year?

$40,000 – pretty good in anybody's book.

But the tactics to take out the right loan aren't that simple. It's critical to know the difference between bad and good loans because a poor loan can turn your investment upside down.

Good vs Bad Debt (and Why the Debt You Leverage for Property Is the Good Kind)

Generally, good debt is the money you own on assets or investments that help you accumulate wealth in the long run. For instance, business and student loans, as well as mortgages, are considered good debt.

Bad debt, however, is defined as the funds you borrow without improving your finances. Consumer loans and credit cards are excellent examples of bad debt.

But this brief disambiguation of bad vs good debt is too simple. The debt game is much more nuanced, and it's worth looking into it to understand all the rules.

Student Loans

Those who don't come from affluent families usually need to take out a student loan to get a good college education.

But not all college degrees are equal, and that's why a borrower needs to be really careful about choosing the right college program. The rule is that you shouldn't borrow more than what you'll earn in the first year after getting hired.

To put that into context, if you're after a master's degree and it can give you an average salary of $70,000 a year, it's wise not to get a student loan higher than that.

The logic behind this strategy is that your salary will be increasing in the coming years. That allows you to cover the interest rate on your student loan. Plus, you'll be able to repay the loan in full within the designated timeframe without jeopardising your cash flow and personal finance.

However, some are afraid that the economy might be shaky by the time they graduate and, therefore, choose to be less in debt.

That kind of mindset is perfectly fine, but you can't really predict if the job market is going to be unstable a few years from now. That being said, it's advisable to minimise what you owe in student loans as much as possible.

But property loans and mortgages are a bit different, which makes them less of a risk.

Mortgages

If you were to track down the history of mortgages, it's easy to understand that they're among the safest forms of borrowing.

Why?

Because the monthly mortgage payments ultimately add equity to your property. But the strategy to take advantage of a mortgage isn't that straightforward.

The 2008 mortgage crisis and recession clearly showed that prices can't go up indefinitely. And you need to know precisely what you're doing when borrowing money against your property.

For example, ARMs (Adjustable-Rate Mortgages) are among the terms you need to fully understand before taking the plunge. Otherwise, you could be adding risk to your investment.

But allow me to make it clear – I'm not trying to scare you or anything. My goal is to point you in the right direction and help you avoid the mistakes inexperienced investors make.

And again, it's best to look at some numbers so you understand what to do.

Your monthly mortgage should be about 28% of your total monthly income, preferably even less than that. And the percentage should include lender mortgage insurance (LMI). Also, you need to pay attention to the loan terms.

For instance, the ARMs above allow for a lower interest rate at the start. But they can rise, and you could end up paying much more than expected.

Sure, that kind of monthly payment increase shouldn't jeopardise your investment. However, it could limit your cash flow and returns.

What is the No. 1 Question for Property Investors?

To cut to the chase, the No. 1 question is if your debt is going to bring in more than you invested.

So, how do you come up with the correct answer?

For one, it's vital to look closely at interest payment, principal repayment, then consider alternative uses of the borrowed funds.

Knowing all that, you need to figure out if the debt works for you based on your current finances. The goal is to get a ballpark estimate if you'd be getting all your money back and earn some on top of it.

Of course, with the right property investments, you'll surely get the money back and earn substantial interest. But still, you need to ask this question and assess your debt to ensure it's not too much of a burden.

How to Use Leverage in Property Investment

As said, leveraging is borrowing funds to invest in a property and mortgage is the means to get that leverage. And this type of loan is really interesting when you allocate the funds towards an investment property.

Why?

When purchasing an investment property, you expect certain returns, ideally right away, as the investor mentioned at the beginning of this chapter. Therefore, you need to create a leveraging strategy that amplifies potential return.

To make sense of the mechanisms behind leveraging strategy, it's best to look closely at its two main benefits – ROI (Return on Investment) and Quantity of Investments.

#1 – ROI

Say you found a great rental property and the asking price is $100,000, and you have that much to invest. Then, we'll assume you can rent that property for $1,000 per month.

If you choose not to leverage, the property will cost you $100,000 plus the monthly expenses. For example, we'll set the monthly costs at $250 in total.

So, how much of a cash flow does this property bring in every month?

The maths is simple; it's $750.

But what if you choose to leverage and take out a mortgage?

The common down payment on a mortgage is 20%, meaning you'll need to spend only $20,000 to get the property. Sure, you'll need to pay the mortgage every month, but that shouldn't be a big deal.

With a typical interest rate of about 5%, that mortgage payment could be about $430 per month. Yes, it might be higher depending on the duration of the loan, but let's stick with the given number.

So, the expenses are $250, combine that with the mortgage payment and it's easy to calculate that the leveraged property would bring in $320 per month.

The cash flow is much smaller than without leverage. But remember, you're an investor and the goal is to get the highest possible returns on the money you invest.

Now, we need to use the cash-on-cash equation to determine the difference in returns.

The equation is: your net monthly income multiplied by 12 months then divided by the initial investment. Next, you multiply the number by 100 to get the percentage. Here's what the equation looks like in different scenarios.

If you pay the full amount without the leverage, the equation is as follows:

$(750 \times 12)/100{,}000 = 0.09 \times 100 = 9\%$

So, you get 9% returns, which is decent. But what percentage do you get if you leverage?

$(320 \times 12)/20{,}000 = 0.192 \times 100 = 19.2\%$

At this point, you understand that it's possible to more than double your returns if you use leverage. The point is that the cash flow means very little if you fail to factor in the initial investment.

That being said, not all leveraged property investments bring in double-digit, cash-on-cash returns. But when you know how to run the numbers, it's easy to gauge which property has the potential for the highest returns.

#2 – *Quantity of Investments*

Again, let's say you have $100,000 to invest and you choose to leverage.

In the leveraging scenario above, we spent only $20,000 on a down payment for one property, leaving $80,000 unallocated. So, you have money for four additional investment properties, assuming the down payment is $20,000.

That allows you to get five properties instead of one (when you pay for a property in full). And this doesn't mean you'll be increasing the risk five times. Rather, you'll be able to reap all the benefits.

The most obvious benefit is that you'll get a much greater monthly cash flow. If the monthly return is the same for all the properties, you're looking at $1,600 ($320 x 5) in recurring income. But let's run that through the cash-on-cash equation:

$(1{,}600 \times 12)/10{,}000 = 0.192 \times 100 = 19.2\%$

But it gets even better. When applicable, you can expect significant increases in the appreciation benefits.

Also, you can make savings due to tax benefits which tend to be pretty high on rental properties. More importantly, choosing to leverage and purchasing five properties actually help you mitigate risk.

How?

Having five properties diversifies your real estate portfolio. It means that you could choose one wrong property and still have a decent cash flow and yield to offset potential losses.

In Leverage We Trust

By leveraging and being smart when choosing your properties, you can build an outstanding real estate portfolio pretty fast.

But note that the numbers given in hypothetical scenarios are just there to illustrate the point, not hint at how much you should be spending.

Anyway, the main takeaway is that you now know the strategy to use debt to grow your property portfolio. Plus, you know the equation that helps you determine if it makes sense to leverage a specific property.

However, you might not want to jump right into five different properties if you're a novice. And that's the reason why you should determine exactly where you are on your property investment journey.

CHAPTER 4

The Different Stages in Your Property Investment Journey

Previously, we talked about good and bad debt, and we explored a case study of my client, an experienced investor. But property is excellent for beginner investors as well. If for nothing else than the low risk and high potential for capital growth.

So, I'd like to share another client story. This time, it's about first-time investors whose goal was to grow their superannuation through capital growth and positive cash flow.

Given the requirements, my task was to find a property that could provide precisely that – positive cash flow and substantial capital growth.

And yes, it might seem like a mission impossible, but we did it.

The right property became available in NSW, about half an hour from Newcastle.

As for the numbers, the client purchased the property for $390,000, and it's currently valued at $440,000. That puts capital growth at 12% or $50,000.

Additionally, the weekly rent at the time of purchase was $450 and the property yield was 6%.

Also, the property was in a really low vacancy rate area (0.8%). Indeed, the competition was tight, but then the client was able to pick and choose their tenants.

If you heard the numbers, without knowing it was a first-time investor, you might have thought that this client had at least a few properties under their belt.

But here's the thing. People who are just starting out in real estate need a property that fits their stage in the investor journey. And my client got exactly that.

To rephrase, it would be wrong to jump right into a negatively-geared property. Or a development where you have to deal with a lot of paperwork and whatnot.

Now, it pays to explore the different stages in this journey to help you understand the strategy to choose real estate based on the stage you're at.

Stage #1 – Accumulation

In the accumulation stage, investors are supposed to build an asset base. That base should give them enough equity to grow their wealth. Therefore, this stage is not focused on increasing your income but on searching for real estate with high capital growth.

Why is this so?

I suspect your ultimate goal is to build passive income. Also, you'd want to begin building a property portfolio that would help you easily transition to the next stage.

To do so, you need to look for real estate that meets specific criteria.

As mentioned, you need to purchase properties that create high capital growth because, in turn, that builds equity. Then, from equity, you gain passive income to secure your financial freedom and set the stage for growing your portfolio further.

Furthermore, you can use both the real estate equity and the passive income to get enough funds for a really comfortable retirement.

How?

The idea is to look for the so-called A-grade properties. For example, this means that you should purchase rental properties where the tenants have enough disposable income.

Why?

By having enough disposable income, the tenants should be okay with raising rental prices. That's because their salaries will be rising as well, and the tenants want to continue living in an area that's high in demand.

The property from the introductory story is like that. The vacancy rate was relatively low due to the rising demand and the favourable characteristics of the area. And when you think about it, the strategy is quite simple.

High demand drives capital growth, so it boosts capital growth and your equity.

Also, you should note that the accumulation stage doesn't end overnight. For some investors, the stage might take up to 15 years.

Of course, I'm here to help you minimise that time as much as possible. However, choosing the right property and building your portfolio takes time, and it depends on many different factors.

The important thing is to get you off the ground and create enough equity to start buying a new property every couple of years, for example.

Lastly, I'd like to go back to A-grade properties and stress that they should outperform the market by providing immediate rental income and high capital growth. And the demographics of a particular area are critical because it draws in specific people.

On that note, you shouldn't make the mistake of refusing to buy a property just because you wouldn't want to live there. Your opinion in this respect is unimportant if the property ticks all the right boxes.

Stage #2 – Consolidation

In this stage, the goal is to minimise the loan-to-value ratio as much as possible. This is assuming that you leveraged the properties instead of buying everything out of pocket.

You'll be doing this to mitigate the risk and lower the portfolio debt. Consequently, your cash flow will increase, allowing you to grow the portfolio even further.

To lower the rate, you can use one of the four tried and tested methods. And yes, it's okay to combine them.

Method #1 – Not Adding More Properties

If you refrain from buying, the debt in your portfolio naturally gets lower. That is, the loan-to-value ratio will get lower.

This is because the capital growth will continue increasing, boosting the value of the entire asset base. Plus, you'll probably manage to pay off one or more properties in total.

Method #2 – Using Savings Products

You should consider this method only when your current savings products are mature enough.

To explain, you can use the money from your pension fund, retirement annuity sum, or an investment fund (if you have one) to channel cash into a property portfolio.

Ideally, this would allow for a debt-free portfolio, and you'll end up with millions of dollars' worth of property to play around with.

Method #3 – Sell, Sell, Sell

Okay, I'm exaggerating here a bit to illustrate my point. This doesn't mean you should sell a huge chunk of the portfolio.

But you may want to consider selling one or two of the assets to cover the debt on the rest of the portfolio. At best, you'll still have some free cash left to reinvest or spend the earnings as you see fit.

Method #4 – Use Disposable Income

If there's any extra cash lying around, why not use it to cover the debt on your portfolio?

And I'm not suggesting you should compensate your lifestyle choices to lessen portfolio debt. But whenever there's some money you don't know how to allocate, it's best to minimise debt.

Again, this move would allow you to further lower the risk and boost your cash flow.

As you proceed on the investor journey, you'll find that one or more methods perfectly fit your current financial position and investment strategy.

And you shouldn't think twice about doing the right thing because it'll pay off immensely in the long run.

Stage #3 – Generating Passive Income

I've already talked about passive income, but it's helpful to revisit the topic and view it from a different perspective.

Getting to the passive income stage means you can comfortably live off the cash flow generated from your property portfolio. This is what many of you have strived for since the very beginning – to create enough income to replace the income you get from your day job.

And when that happens, you have a couple of options at your disposal.

For instance, you can choose to repay all the debt in the portfolio and live just on passive income. But note that you'll be forgoing the taxation and leverage benefits when you do that.

Still, this is an excellent position to be in because there won't be any financial burden on your portfolio.

Should you choose a less conservative route, you can cover the portfolio debt only to secure an optimal loan-to-value ratio. By doing that, you'll retain some taxation benefits and leverage while still having an excellent passive income.

Stage #4 – Creating Legacy

Before this stage, you have already created an outstanding property portfolio with little to no debt. This means that you've accumulated enough wealth to secure a great financially free retirement.

Also, the legacy stage is where you start considering how to use the portfolio to make your family financially stable in the years to come. Plus, you might want to provide support to institutions or charities.

Ultimately, this is the stage all of us dream about.

Why?

This is when you're a veteran property investor and begin to look back at your achievements. Knowing that you have the power to make a difference in the world and your family instils a sense of pride and accomplishment that's hard to rival.

And in many ways, the legacy stage is your moment to shine.

That's when you have enough equity to make everyone happy and make an impact on your community, if not the world. But it's not about the money alone.

Yes, having the funds to do whatever you want helps. However, this is where all your experience, wisdom, and strategies get to shine.

But let me explain.

As some veteran investors call it, the legacy stage is a "fluid state". This means that you can do anything you want with your assets. And it's not uncommon for investors to start accumulating again when they reach this stage.

It's perfectly fine to go back into the game at stage one. But I suspect that you'd want to leave something behind so that future generations remember you.

Because of that, it's best to give the legacy stage careful thought and come up with a strategy that best fits you and your family.

I'm sure you'll have more than enough to secure your retirement and family. So, why not give back to your community, even if you choose to go into the accumulation stage again.

This is how you ensure that you and your family's name is remembered by generations to come.

What's Your Stage?

Why do you need to understand the stage in your property investor journey?

Simply because it informs your decisions and strategies to grow or improve your portfolio. And it helps you to know how to overcome property investment challenges to remain in the game for the long haul.

Arguably, the accumulation stage is the most critical because you're building an asset base and moving towards passive income. That stage also bears the most risk because it's essential to purchase suitable properties and avoid financial bottlenecks.

This chapter should have provided you with enough information to avoid repeating the same mistakes I did.

However, if you're at the very beginning of the journey, nailing the first property is paramount. Not only does it boost your motivation, but it also removes much of the stress from the property game.

This is why I choose to dedicate the entire next chapter to getting your first property.

CHAPTER 5

Getting Your First Property (and the Crippling Mistakes Most People Make)

In the last chapter, we ended with the idea that you need to make the first property count. And if you do that right, every other property you purchase should follow the same investment strategy and goals.

But getting that first property right isn't as easy as it might appear.

No worries, I'm here to provide guidance and share a success story that will help you get a clear picture of what to look for.

Almost $300K in Profit in 12 Months

This is a fantastic story of a married couple who made it big!

They were both nurses and had a lot of knowledge about property investments before coming to me. However, the couple didn't have the time to put theory into practice because of their tight schedule.

To make things more complicated, they had two young children. Therefore, the couple had to work different shifts to ensure one of the parents looked after the youngsters.

Needless to say, that kind of hectic schedule left almost no time to look for property investments.

Their story reminded me of my own, so I made it my mission to help them.

The couple wanted to keep their existing house and renovate it because the property had a lot of intrinsic value. Namely, the couple's goal was to build three more villas at the back of their house and bring their portfolio to four properties.

The location for doing that was ideal. The land was in Tasmania, in the centre of the town, close to all the amenities. Even better, developing the land would give the couple the benefit of multiple exit strategies.

For example, they could keep all of the houses and rent them for passive income. Or, they could sell the three villas for a profit, keep their home debt-free, and still have some money to reinvest.

Either way, the options were great, and there was almost no risk regardless of what they chose. But note that this client already had DA approval to build the three villas at the back.

Now, let's look at the numbers.

We managed to drive the asking price from $345,000 to $325,000, saving the client $20,000. The rental of their current home, while waiting for construction and approvals, was $350 per week with a 5.6% return.

That looked really promising, but the real money was in the projected profit.

After constructing and selling the villas, the couple should be cashing in $285,000 in profit in only 12 months.

And I assure you, there's no reason you can't emulate their success.

Getting Prepared to Invest in Property – The Seven Steps to Take

Step #1 – Getting Clear on Your Goals

You need to be realistic about the property investment game and base your goals on your current financial position. I mean, you should be sure that the venture fits your current life and business circumstances.

But, as evident from the case study above, business circumstances could be tricky. Though there's very little to worry about if you get the right help and have a great starting position to begin with.

Step #2 – Research

Knowing your goals and financial standing, it's time to start doing the research for the right property. This is the tricky part because it could take much more time than expected, particularly for first-time investors.

Sure, I can help you cut that time and make the right decision. But you should also know where and what kind of property to go for. Naturally, you're looking for an A-grade option with immense capital growth potential.

Step #3 – Budgeting

I believe that you'll be going for the leveraging strategy, so you need to keep in mind that the lenders will ask you for a 10%–20% deposit. Simply, you need to have some cash up front to get the ball rolling, and it's not only for the deposit.

When venturing into property investments, the incurring fees usually include the following:

- Conveyancing and legal fees
- Maintenance
- Stamp duty
- Borrowing interest
- Insurance

Additionally, this is where you need to factor in variable interest rates on your loan. Maybe, it would be better to go for a split or fixed interest rate loan to avoid limiting your cash flow in the future.

Step #4 – Credit History and Timeframe

Your credit history has to be pristine to get a mortgage or a loan. This is why you should comb through the credit card reports and ensure there's no outstanding debt or errors.

In all frankness, this could be among the most critical steps, and you should do it well before you start looking for properties. Thereon, you need to set a timeframe to save enough money for a deposit.

Step #5 – Property Management

Assuming you've successfully completed the previous steps and got a property, someone needs to manage it.

Like a lot of my clients, you're probably strapped for time, or the property could be far away from your home. To prevent potential problems, it's best to appoint a property manager. The manager's fee would be much lower than trying to fix a poorly managed property.

Step #6 – Insurance

Property insurance isn't an unnecessary expense but a great way to mitigate risk and act proactively against potential problems.

Be it repairs, natural disasters, or rental income protection, insurance is the best way to safeguard your investment.

That's why you should take the time to choose the policy that will cover everything you need.

Insurance premiums may vary widely, and not all insurers provide the same terms.

Step #7 – Small Things to Include in Your Budget

On top of the deposit and investment fees, there are many other small expenses to factor in. These should pose a financial burden, but they add up quickly if you fail to budget them in time.

They include:

- Council and water rates
- Vacancy cost
- Advertising

- Lost rental cost
- Miscellaneous recurring charges

These Are the Six Mistakes New Investors Make (That You Must Avoid)

Getting adequately prepared is only the beginning. And even if you do everything right, you still need to have the correct investor mindset to avoid getting burned at the very start.

Here are the things to keep in mind:

#1 – Investing With Your Heart

In one of the previous sections, I mentioned that you shouldn't refuse to buy a property just because you wouldn't want to live there.

Much the same way, you shouldn't purchase a property just because you became enamoured by it. Using your heart for decision-making is one of the most dangerous things for any investor.

You need to use logic and carefully weigh all the characteristics of a property to make an informed decision. This is where you need to assess the area demographics, vacancy rates, capital growth potential, and other metrics to make a sound decision.

#2 – Not Planning Properly

Taking the time to plan each and every step saves you a lot of stress in the long run.

Always keep in mind that your goal is to create a lucrative portfolio to give you financial freedom as soon as possible.

On that note, your plan should lay out the strategy to approach the property market exactly like that. Simply, if a particular property doesn't bring you closer to your goals, you shouldn't waste time on it.

Plus, it pays to consider different types of property (developments, subdivision, etc.) and assess their capacity to add to your portfolio.

#3 – *Dithering*

Dithering is among the most common mistakes with first-time investors. They get excited, venture into a property, then never take the next step and invest in another one. And the reasons for this vary.

Some might be too scared, believing the risk is too high. Others make the wrong choice the first time round and lose all motivation to proceed. But then, there are those who are satisfied with just one investment.

I don't want you to be like any of them.

Your property portfolio has the power to change your life and finance forever. Don't miss the chance to achieve that.

#4 – *Speculation*

Some novice property investors think it's possible to become millionaires fast. That's why they focus too much on short-term gains, trying to squeeze every dollar from their investments.

However, this isn't investing; it's speculation that rarely ends well.

The reality is that it could take more than a decade to build a property portfolio that can give you financial freedom. And yes, you'll be boosting your cash flow in the meantime, but it won't be the millions some expect.

That being said, specific properties might be an excellent quick flip. But remember, you're in it for the long haul, and quick flips may actually hurt your cash flow.

#5 – *Wrong Property*

This is among the most common and most dangerous mistakes.

To stress yet again, you need to look for a cash flow-positive property in a good neighbourhood. Also, that property needs to have the potential for high capital gains. Ideally, you'll be able to rent it out immediately after purchase.

Sure, choosing the right property is more nuanced than that. And by the end of this book, you'll have enough knowledge to pick just the one that fits your goals and current finance.

#6 – Failing at Cash Flow Management

It's not hard to get caught up in the moment and forget to keep track of your cash flow.

And I'm not passing any judgement; it could happen to anyone. But it's vital to stay on top of all the costs involving the purchase and maintenance of a property. If need be, you can ask for advice from a professional accountant or a real estate professional like me.

In addition, some of the previous sections in the book list different fees and expenses associated with your purchase. Therefore, it should be much easier for you to make a list of all the related expenses.

Due Diligence – Why Is It Important to Get This Right Before You Spend Any Money

Property investors use due diligence to mitigate risk and get a complete understanding of the property they're interested in. Plus, due diligence helps them negotiate more effectively.

The due diligence process begins well before you make an offer on a property, and it should encompass several different aspects.

For one, you need to take the time to research the property market. You'll be looking at the location, demand, and rental yield for a particular property.

More importantly, you need to find out if the location is going to be subject to zoning and infrastructure changes. That's vital because it could affect the capital growth of a property.

If all of the above appears fine, you need to inspect the property's structure.

As a rule, the structure needs to be sound if you're to make a good investment. That means you should always have a professional inspection before making an offer. You know, there are properties that look very attractive but turn out to be crumbling on the inside.

Anyway, when you have all the facts about a property, it gives you the upper hand to negotiate the price. Also, keep in mind that there's no room for false information and irrational claims. That goes both for you and the seller.

If you were to use the wrong information, the seller could step down and refuse to do business with you. Similarly, if you see that the seller is basing the offer on false claims, it might be better to look for a different property.

To prevent that, you should create a list of realistic negotiation points based on your research. For example, you may find that the government plans to build infrastructure in the area. That move could boost traffic and decrease the land value.

But when you use the facts in negotiations, it's crucial not to appear too sensational. To do so may cause the real estate agent and the seller to distrust you and ultimately refuse to work with you.

Get Ready for Property Shopping

To recap, you need to take the time and do your homework before purchasing your first property.

As an investor, you need to be clear on your goals, budget, and investment strategy. Also, pay attention to your personal finance and don't forget to factor in all the small things that may affect the property cost.

That will help you prevent some of the most common mistakes investors make. And on that note, we can move on to determine how to actually get your first property.

CHAPTER 6

How to Get Your First Investment Property

I'd like to open this chapter with a fantastic success story.

One of my clients was a budding professional who wanted to start building a property portfolio at a very young age. Like you, this client saw the tremendous potential to accumulate wealth and decided to do that while working two jobs in nursing.

How's that possible? – you may ask.

I helped the client come up with a creative purchasing strategy to achieve the investment goals.

Let's look at the strategy itself.

We found a great property in The Hunter Valley, NSW, and the size of the plot was 850sqm. The strategy was to subdivide the land into two lots. Then, the client decided to renovate the existing home and build another house at the back, using battle-axe access.

After construction, the client wanted to keep the new property and sell the renovated property. The money from selling the property would give the client enough capital to look for another similar or better deal.

But what kind of funds did the client need to make it possible?

The initial asking price for the property was $415,000, and we negotiated it down to $399,000, saving the client $16,000.

The subdivision, renovation, and building cost were $400,000, which matched the intrinsic value of the newly renovated house. But the value of the new house was an impressive $700,000.

The beauty of this deal was that the client started with minimal initial funds and leveraged the property. But after the renovation and construction, the client had a brand-new property and much more cash to reinvest.

This story might sound too good to be true, but any novice investor can achieve the same, if not higher, level of success.

From the previous chapters, you know what mistakes to avoid. Now, we'll explore what you need to do to nail that first property.

Understanding the Market – What You Need to Look for When Investing in Property

To make a profit, you need to purchase a property at the right price, but this could prove challenging.

Why?

Unlike some other assets, properties are tricky to price. I mean, the sellers sometimes have unrealistic expectations, and the markets can suddenly shift.

However, if you play your cards right and research thoroughly, it's possible to purchase the property under the market value. The basic rule is that you shouldn't make an offer until you fully understand the area where a property is located.

But how do you get a complete picture of an area?

Researching into the prices of other properties, vacancy rates, and demographics is a good start. But you'd need more information.

Mortgage insurers and lenders can be a great source of invaluable information on different properties and locations. Do your best to get that information and ask lenders/insurers to assist you in making the right decision.

However, there's one particular thing to keep in mind.

You can get significant tax deductions on investment properties. But you shouldn't purchase a property just because you'll get a deduction. Additionally, you should explore different property classes:

- Houses
- Home units
- Land
- Subdivisions

Depending on the area you're interested in, one property type may outperform another in terms of yield, rental income, and capital gains.

Understandably, this could be too much for you to handle due to your busy schedule. But don't forget that with the right help, everything is possible. After all, the client mentioned at the start of this chapter pulled it off while handling two jobs.

Consider Hiring a Property Manager

The job of a property manager is to keep everything in check for your tenants and you. A great manager will feed you information about the property's performance to help you extract the most value from it.

More importantly, an experienced manager is well-versed in property law. So, you'll always know your responsibilities and rights as a landlord.

The manager can also help you with repairs, maintenance problems, or any other related issue. But you should review all of the issues and approve the incurred expenses. Of course, this doesn't apply to emergencies.

Additionally, a property manager is there to find suitable tenants, check their background, and ensure they aren't late with the rent. You shouldn't deal with the tenants too much because the law protects their position.

However, scheduled property inspections are okay.

The idea is to be sure that a tenant is keeping your investment in good order. And it wouldn't hurt to build a good professional relationship with them.

Now, you might think that a good property manager is expensive, but that's not the case. Commonly, they take a percentage of the rent for providing their services. This fee is tax-deductible, and it's a drop in the ocean compared to the service they provide.

However, even the best of managers can't help if you fail to grasp the market dynamics and financing of your investment.

Market Dynamics and Financing

I already mentioned that you need to thoroughly research the location, and market dynamics is a vital part of that research.

To figure out the dynamics, you need to pinpoint the highest-performing areas in a specific location. For example, it's not uncommon that one street in the area is the hottest place to invest. But there are also high-performing locations that might be on a downward path, and you should know about them.

But where do you source all that information?

First, it pays to consult with different real estate agents and check how other properties perform. Then, there are independent websites that provide accurate information on the following:

- Average rent
- Property value
- Suburb reports
- Demographics

When armed with all the data, determine what kind of financing (mortgage) is the most suitable. Feel free to approach different lenders and see what kind of funds and payment plans they offer.

As mentioned, investment properties are tax-deductible. But you already know that there's a cost associated with getting the loan and transferring the asset into your hands.

Choosing the Right Location

Throughout the book, I've stressed the importance of picking the perfect location. And it's high time you learned all the intricacies of that process.

Location scouting should begin after you set the investment budget. There's no point in considering the properties you can't afford.

This is why you should have a discussion with your lender in advance to gauge your borrowing capacity. I'm assuming here that you're going to leverage a property, even if you saved up enough to pay for it in full.

Knowing how much money you have, you need to narrow down the properties that appear promising. Of course, they should be within desired locations and your budget.

If it turns out that you can't buy a home in a particular suburb, for example, it's okay to look at what's available in the neighbouring suburbs. Don't let this tiny failure lower your motivation, you're looking for the best deal available, wherever that might be.

Speaking of suburbs, some investors choose to map them out. This is how they get to know the suburb's popularity and find smaller areas that might rise in price soon. Consequently, investors know which locations have the highest capital growth potential.

And when you know which area is potentially the most lucrative, you need to dig even deeper.

Infrastructure, Lifestyle Attractions, and Other Characteristics

Generally, growing infrastructure will ultimately drive up property prices. But, as stated, it's not always like that.

If the infrastructure is designed to boost traffic, that could deflect potential renters. However, specific infrastructure improvements are engineered to better the lifestyle of an area. So, you should consult with the municipal government to understand their plans.

As for lifestyle attractions, being close to parks, nature, shopping malls, and other amenities is a plus. You should keep in mind that certain suburbs could be far away from these, but they usually have additional features that make them highly desirable.

For instance, CBD and water views are major selling points in certain areas. To put this into context, I'll use the example of Seaford in Victoria.

The properties that are close to the beach are usually $100,000 more expensive than those close to the freeway. This isn't likely to change. In fact, beachside real estate has been getting more expensive, and it's remained largely unaffected by the downturns in other areas of the property market.

But even if you manage to get a beachside property, it needs to have excellent access to transportation. That's also important for suburbs because they appreciate more in value if they're well connected with the rest of the city.

As a rule, the property you get needs easy access to freeways and major roads. Availability of public transportation is a plus. You need to keep in mind that your renters might want different options to commute to work.

Lastly, when choosing the right location, you should be careful with the locals. I mean, they can be a great source of information, but some are naysayers who dislike investors per se. That's another reason you need to focus only on the realistic data and location assessment, not on what somebody's saying.

Getting Your Property Loan – How to Prepare the Perfect Application

The key questions investors ask are:

- What qualifies me for investment loans?
- What amount can I borrow?

When you know the answers to these questions, you can prepare for the application stress-free. Plus, you get a clear picture of your capacity to finance a property investment.

You already know it's necessary to place a 20% deposit. Some lenders might allow for less, but 20% is the figure you should be working with. In reality, few lenders would finance more than 80% of your investment, particularly when you're a first-time investor.

Also, you need to know that you can't take out an investment loan to cover the deposit.

At best, you've saved up enough to cover the deposit and have kept that money in a bank for three months or more. And it goes without saying that you need to have a spotless credit card history and credit rating.

Lastly, stable employment and sizeable income show the lenders that you can cover repayments and mortgage. But what about professional investors whose only job is property?

They need to provide tax documents and bank statements to prove they're financially stable. Afterwards, banks will approve their mortgage much the same way they do yours.

But is there anything else you can do to prepare yourself for getting your first investment property?

If you're financially stable and submit all the necessary documents, there shouldn't be a problem getting your mortgage approved. But real estate is also a mindset game.

No matter how much you prepare, buying your first property is daunting. But it's critical to keep the emotions out of the equation and keep focusing on your priorities. The best way to make the process less stressful is to keep going back to the numbers.

As mentioned a few times before, you need to ensure you're buying a cash flow-positive property with high capital gain potential. Additionally, don't forget to consider your current financial capabilities even before you start shopping for a mortgage.

The last thing you want is to get all the paperwork ready, find the perfect property, then get refused because you're already in too much debt.

But I don't want this to scare you; I'm here to provide all the assistance you need and ascertain whether you're doing the right things every step of the way.

Ready, Steady, Buy

At the end of the day, buying your first property involves a few steps, and there are a bunch of things to keep in mind.

Right now, the entire process might seem overwhelming…

But remember, you're not in it alone. And when you ace your first investment property, the next one will be much easier to handle.

The important thing is to apply the same property/location assessment strategies to find the next best deal. Plus, you shouldn't fall for the trappings of negatively-geared investments, no matter how promising they might seem. But this topic merits a chapter of its own.

CHAPTER 7

Why Negative Gearing Is a Bad Investment Strategy

Picture a client who doesn't have any investment knowledge. To make the deal more complicated, imagine their budget is limited.

The client story I'd like to share here is exactly like that.

Nevertheless, this client was after property with high capital growth. And, of course, they were looking for a cash flow-positive property.

Why?

If the property wasn't cash flow positive, that would put additional strain on their budget. Also, any major renovation upgrades could extend the time it took for the property to start providing a stable cash flow.

So, the client wanted to buy a brand-new property and capitalise on depreciation claims. Additionally, their goal was to avoid any unexpected maintenance issues.

Now, getting such a property at a bargain may appear a bit far-fetched. But nothing is impossible.

After thorough research, we found just the right property in the South Coast, NSW. The property was a Torrens titled duplex located in New Torrens.

But the beauty of this deal is obvious when you know the numbers.

The client got the property for $420,000, and it's currently valued at $470,000. In other words, the property had a capital growth of $50,000 or 11% of the purchase price in one year of purchase.

Given the client's lack of knowledge and money, that's an outstanding achievement.

But let's look at more numbers.

The weekly rental return is $450, and the annual rental return is 5.6% of the property value. Combine that with the fact that the duplex is in an area with a 1.2% vacancy rate, and it's safe to assume that the rental returns are only going to grow.

Okay, this client might need to tackle some competition down the line and consider renovation and improvements. But since the capital growth is so high, that shouldn't be too much of an issue.

Now, what would have happened if this client got a negatively-geared property?

First of all, they wouldn't get good rental returns, and their maintenance costs would've been pretty high.

Also, they would probably need to go above and beyond to get the property on the market, to rent or sell it. And the long-term capital growth might not cover all the investments.

To give you the complete picture of negative gearing, this whole chapter is dedicated to just that.

What Is Negative Gearing and How Does It Work?

Assuming you're leveraging a property (borrowing money to finance it), the goal is to find a deal where property income exceeds your monthly mortgage payment. That's what we call a positively-geared property.

But you shouldn't only factor in the mortgage repayments. The rental income needs to exceed additional expenses such as water rates, strata levies, council fees, etc. Of course, this is only the case if the given fees are applicable.

Anyway, you could end up out of pocket if the property is negatively geared.

However, the deal with negatively-geared properties is not strictly black and white. And it's not like you're going to end up bankrupt if you purchase one such property.

I mean, there are tax deductions that allow you to offset the rental loss incurred in one year. And, you can offset it from your other income – such as your salary, for example.

That sounds much better, but take a moment to think about negative gearing.

Do you want a property that can't cover the expenses of your investment and doesn't leave you with some earnings?

I bet you don't.

However, there are investors who appear to be doing just fine with negatively-geared properties. Though, the strategies they're using may not apply to novice investors or people who are still growing their portfolio.

Why?

Simply because they don't have the time, money, or expertise to pivot those properties and remain in the black. Also, the tax deductions might not cover everything that's been lost on a particular property.

The Four Reasons Why Negative Gearing Is a Bad Idea for a New Investor

The previous section touched upon some of the reasons, but it's critical you understand this properly. So, we should delve deeper into it.

#1 – Negative Effect on the Cash Flow

When you have to keep covering the property expenses month after month, you're cementing yourself into your current job.

Like me, many of my clients worked two jobs to be solvent enough to enter the real estate game. More importantly, all of them strive for financial freedom and wealth.

But how can you attract wealth if you need to throw money left and right to make ends meet?

Still, some investors are ready to lose money, believing property's capital growth will cover all that. However, this is a speculative strategy and, as a new investor, you can never be certain if the capital growth meets your expectations.

Negative gearing slows you from building your property portfolio faster, as there is no disposable income left to be able to borrow and buy more assets.

Also, the stress of dealing with a negatively-geared property might kill your motivation to invest more.

#2 – *Borrowing Money Against Equity*

To offset some of the expenses of negatively-geared properties, investors borrow even more money. That puts some cash in their pockets, but realistically they're only exacerbating the problem.

But let me give you the context so you know how this works.

Say there's some capital growth in a negatively-geared property and you want to take advantage of it. You go to a lender and borrow money against that particular equity.

On the surface, that doesn't sound like a bad idea because you could get cash to invest more.

But think about it again.

Effectively, you're borrowing against the asset that's the most expensive for you. Therefore, you're limiting the ability to have a stable cash flow even further.

To stress, with negatively-geared properties, there's a risk you won't move beyond investment property number one.

Why?

Because you won't be able to afford to buy the next one. And this ties back to losing your motivation to grow as a property investor and ultimately gain financial freedom.

#3 – What Happens if the Markets Go Down?

If the markets go down, you go down with them.

Okay, I'm being pessimistic, and it's usually not that abysmal. However, stagnant markets can also limit your ability to grow your property portfolio and make money.

And if that persists long enough, you might be compelled to sell off your negatively-geared property at a loss. Then, you could be worse off compared to when you started.

But don't stress about it; we won't let that happen.

Is Negative Gearing Ever a Good Idea?

Right off the bat, negative gearing is rarely a good idea.

Buying a negatively-geared property means that you have more than enough income to keep holding the property despite losing money.

Basically, this strategy is for those affluent enough to cover the cost of the property without getting into more debt.

And yes, if you hold a property for quite some time, it's bound to increase in value. This applies assuming you've bought it in the right location, at the right time, and for the right price, even if it's negatively geared.

But can you be certain about your choices?

No, not really. Particularly, not with negatively-geared properties.

The markets can turn, and you won't have the time or money to wait until the storm is over.

Okay, I mentioned that there are tax returns for negatively-geared properties. That could help you keep your head above the water, but these tax benefits don't work for everybody.

Generally, the given deductions are for high-income individuals. More specifically, those who already pay more than 40% tax on their income. Plus, you need to factor in asset depreciation and a bunch of other stuff.

On the other hand, when you're working with a relatively small asset base, the tax returns aren't likely to help you turn a negatively-geared property into a positive one.

Lastly, some investors go for a negatively-geared property because renovation and development give them instant equity.

This strategy is okay, but it's not for first-time investors.

Why?

You need to get the property for a bargain, and the location has to have exceptionally high growth potential. Meeting these two parameters is a huge challenge in its own right.

Then, you also need to calculate the cost of renovation and development. Plus, you need to be sure that your property won't sit on the market for too long.

So, realistically, you can expect instant equity only with positively-geared properties.

Gear Your Properties Properly

The idea of getting a negatively-geared property at a bargain and associated tax benefits may sound alluring. But I'd strongly advise against it.

This book aims to help you prevent some of the mistakes I made and the mistakes common to novice property investors.

Also, there's hardly a better thing than an investment that starts bringing in some cash as soon as you put money into it. It does wonders for your motivation and helps start building a portfolio that will ultimately lead to the financial freedom you strive for.

And the great thing is that you might not need to wait too long to get that.

How?

Keep on reading to find out.

CHAPTER 8

How to Fast Track Your Investments Using Property Professionals

Here, I'd like to open with a client story I'm particularly proud of.

The client I'm referring to is a single mum who wanted to secure a better, more financially stable life for her children.

She saw property investment as one of the best ways to do that, and she wanted to invest in her super. But like many of my clients, she had no prior knowledge of real estate.

Anyway, she was referred to us by a friend whom we also helped invest in real estate using super.

So, what was the strategy to help this single mum?

As always, we were looking for a cash flow-positive property with excellent capital growth potential. Additionally, it had to be in a high population growth area where there are multiple jobs available.

But we managed to get something even better than that.

Using our methodology, we found an area in NSW experiencing a property boom due to affordable house prices. The access to major amenities by road transport networks and rail also contributed to the attractiveness of that particular location.

Knowing all that, you might think the client had to pay the list price for the property, but no, we negotiated a fantastic deal.

The asking price was $435,000, but she ended up paying $420,000, saving the client $15,000.

Even better, the property's LVR was 70%, and the weekly rental was $520 at the time of purchase. And the vacancy rate was 0.75%, allowing the client to quickly find renters and start bringing in some cash.

Finally, the projected yearly growth was 7.5%, so it's not hard to calculate how much she'll earn down the line.

But the critical thing is that this single mum couldn't have landed such a great deal without professional help.

Getting on the Right Track

Considering the long-term earnings, spending your money on an investment property is a no-brainer. By and large, the financial rewards more than justify the money you put in.

Even so, there are people who are apprehensive about spending more to hire a buyer's agent.

To ease some of the apprehension, the following sections will tell you exactly how these agents help and how to choose one.

But before we discuss that, I'd like to expand upon the debate further to help you understand why you need to work with a professional.

With property investments, there are little to no guarantees. And if you just superficially look at the data about a particular location, you might get a false impression that it's a good investment opportunity.

There are a number of parameters that affect a property's capital growth potential and quality. Therefore, it's critical to conduct proper due diligence to avoid getting burnt on your first investment.

But do you have the time and the expertise to do due diligence?

Most likely, you don't, and this is where buyer's agents can be of great help. One of their primary roles is to give you guidance and advice on where and how to invest in real estate.

Simply put, buyer's agents tell you if the time and price are suitable to buy a particular property. Consequently, choosing to work with a buyer's agent may save you a lot of money on your initial investment.

Not only that, but it could also earn you hundreds of thousands in the long run.

Still, there are a few things to keep in mind when working with a buyer's agent.

Get Your Long-Term Goals Straight

Before you approach an agent, you need to be sure about what you want to achieve in the long run.

Why?

Because that's the first thing an agent is going to ask about. And it's not enough just to tell the person you want financial freedom and wealth. Your goals have to be more specific than that.

Start by setting your investment budget and a ballpark timeframe to achieve the goals. For instance, you may have $100,000 to invest, and you want to have ten properties in ten years.

Then, you've already learned that it's essential to go after capital growth and cash flow-positive properties. Or, you might want to consider subdivisions and renovations to add even more value to your investment.

Either way, these are the things your buyer's agent should know about because it helps narrow down the search for the right property.

But even if you're not sure about subdivisions, renovations, and the like, the agent still needs to know your budget and timeframe. That will inform the agency's purchasing strategy to help you take full advantage of your money.

Also, the buyer's agent's job is to guide you through the negotiation process.

Keep in mind that there's a lot of excitement and stress when you're making an offer. And if there's no one to help you mitigate the stress and ease the excitement, you could lose a lot of money.

Remember, I overpaid a lot for one of the properties I bought when starting out. It was partly because of the excitement and partially because I failed to conduct proper due diligence.

And lastly, a buyer's agent is there to safeguard you from misleading real estate agents that underquote.

When the market is booming, like in the story at the beginning of this chapter, underquoting could deprive you of a chance to invest.

How to Find the Right Buyer's Agent

Experience, rapport, and a verifiable track record are vital, but they aren't the only thing.

You should also know that there are different kinds of agents. Based on their speciality and client pool, one agent may suit you better than another, assuming they are both experienced.

But a lot of buyer's agents don't have a speciality – they deal with real estate in general. You're likely to benefit more from an agent niched in rental homes, subdivisions, first-time buyers, etc.

Therefore, you need to do your homework and dig deep to find the right professionals. And since you're investing, the agent needs to have the capacity to walk you through the financial analytics to ensure you're making a good profit.

Plus, you need to find a professional with all the necessary licenses and qualifications. As for their experience, it's best to go with an agent who's been in the business for at least a decade.

On top of that, make sure to work with an agent who charges a fixed fee rather than the percentage of a purchase price. Otherwise, the agent might not be incentivised enough to negotiate the best price for you.

With that in mind, it pays to consider some of the negative aspects of working with a buyer's agent since these mostly have to do with choosing the right person.

Most buyer's agents used to be real estate agents, which isn't bad per se. It means that they have the knowledge to transact in the property market, but they don't necessarily have the investment expertise.

That being said, these agents certainly know how to distinguish a suitable property from a bad one. But you should be looking for an agent who understands investments as well.

The most alarming thing is property spruikers, who sometimes pretend to be buyer's agents. They often try to charge you a membership fee for their services, and when you see that, don't think twice about looking elsewhere.

But buyer's agents aren't the only professionals you should be working with. Mortgage brokers are also of immense help, and that's why I dedicated the next section to their services.

Benefits of Mortgage Brokers

Being a middleman between the banks and you, mortgage brokers have the capacity to get the loan that perfectly fits your current finances.

How?

Mortgage brokers spend a chunk of their time researching the financial market and products to single out the best deals. They have access to a vast pool of available loans and work with financial institutions to help you go through the process quickly.

Another benefit is that they know the ins and outs of the paperwork involved, so you'll be clear on the conditions and terms of the deal before signing a contract.

However, one of the critical benefits is that mortgage brokers usually have flexible work hours. Some will be willing to work on the weekends or evenings at a place that's suitable for you.

This is an immense benefit, especially if you work full time or have family commitments. Just imagine how arduous your application process would become if you had to prepare for the settlement and application yourself.

There's research, mortgage offer comparison, pre-approval, and a lot of other paperwork. However, a broker has a system to do all that for you and keep you in the loop until the deal is closed.

Consequently, you'll have the time to focus on locating an ideal investment opportunity and create a winning strategy to grow your portfolio. But an experienced broker can also give you investment advice related to your loan.

And finally, the fee for their services is well worth the money, given how much value they bring to the table.

Assemble Your Property Investment Team

By now, you know your team should consist of a buyer's agent and a mortgage broker. And you understand how to find and work with these professionals.

But are there any other experts you should consider?

Even though this chapter might lead you to believe real estate agents are unimportant, working with an experienced real estate agent is beneficial. If for nothing else than finding the best investment opportunities when they present themselves in the market.

Then, depending on the property you get, you might also want to involve a property manager. And the same goes for property and insurance agents and property inspectors.

I know that this seems like you're just adding more cost to your investments, but it's not like that. You don't want to leave any stones unturned if you're to make a good profit.

It's not like you're throwing money out of the window; the team is there to protect your investment.

CHAPTER 9

Property Types – Which One to Aim For

Choosing the right property type based on your goals, strategy, and budget can make or break your investment opportunity.

To cast a revealing light on how important property type is, I'd like to share another client story.

This client was a very busy medical practitioner who had no time and expertise to research property developments.

But there's a silver lining.

The client had a lot of equity to invest in brick and mortar and understood how lucrative the deal could be. Also, they had the money to invest in a property consultant who'd spearhead the deal from start to finish.

So, this is almost an ideal client from a property consultant's perspective. But what kind of property type would fit such an investor?

My tactic was to give this client a multiple-strategy deal that could maximise the return on investment and property yield potential.

Therefore, we decided to go for a subdivision into three lots. And soon enough, we found a suitable property in NSW, just 50km from Liverpool CBD.

The land itself was enormous, covering 1,500sqm and included an existing house.

We decided to renovate the house, then subdivide everything into three lots and sell it off. To be exact, we'd sell the renovated house and the two remaining blocks of land.

Now, you might think that the whole deal cost an arm and a leg, but you'd be wrong.

The asking price was $490,000 and the seller understood the value of it. So, we managed to shave off only $5,000 from the asking price, settling at $485,000. It's not too much, but it was better than nothing.

Be that as it may, the cost of renovation, acquisitions, and subdivisions was $200,000, making the total investment $685,000.

I know these numbers seem huge, but you still don't know what we sold the property for.

The smaller block of land with the renovated house went for $400,000. But each of the remaining lots was sold for $300,000 ($600,000 in total).

So how much money did this client make?

To save you the calculation, it was $315,000 and the whole deal got wrapped up in only eight months.

There's no reason you couldn't achieve the same level of success within the same timeframe. The only critical thing is to know what property type to aim for.

The Types

The property types include apartments, stand-alone houses, duplexes, townhouses, commercial properties, and more. From here on, we'll be exploring each property type in detail to give you a better idea of which option best fits your goals, finances, and strategy.

#1 – Apartments

Since my expertise lies in investments other than apartments, I won't spend too much time explaining this property type. But from an investment standpoint, it pays to understand the apartment market as well.

So, you should avoid investing in new apartment buildings, even though it may sound counterintuitive.

Why?

These are usually in high-rise buildings with a relatively large number of units. Add small communal spaces, potential parking problems, and the abundance of similar options in the market, and it's clear that apartments don't provide the capital growth you're aiming to get.

However, if you find a deal in an older apartment building that's 60 or more years old, it's possible to get decent capital growth. But these usually require a lot of renovation, most of which goes to getting the utilities up to today's standards.

Compared to houses, apartments have been performing a bit better from 2018 up until the COVID-19 pandemic. But then, people's lifestyle habits changed, and a lot of professionals will still be working from home even after the pandemic.

Due to that, high-income renters will be looking for more space and peace and quiet in the suburbs because their daily commute is no longer an issue. And if you look at how the property market has performed in Australia in 2020 and 2021, you'll surely spot this trend.

#2 – Stand-Alone Houses

This is a traditional dwelling where you'll be purchasing the land as well as the house.

Since they offer more privacy and flexibility, stand-alone houses are the most popular in Australia, both for investors and renters/homeowners.

Aside from providing an excellent investment opportunity, houses give you the benefit of additional space. They need to have specific block sizes as predetermined by the Australian government, which are generally pretty big.

The interior is often larger compared to townhouses, making your investment more interesting to potential renters. Plus, stand-alone houses usually have a lot of outdoor space and may come on a piece of land suitable for subdivision.

Lastly, the key benefit of investing in a stand-alone house is capital growth. As indicated, the trend shows that this property type appreciates the most, giving you the cash flow to grow your portfolio pretty fast.

#3 – *Duplexes*

Duplexes are among the best investments because they tend to be less expensive than stand-alone houses, and they're quite versatile.

Compared to buying two houses in the same location, a duplex may offer a higher rental yield and a more stable capital growth.

But to truly understand the charm of a duplex, you need to know what exactly it is.

It's a residential home type where you have two units with a division wall in the middle. Often, these units could be on one lot and have one owner. But there are those that are on separate pieces of land and have multiple owners.

Of course, you should avoid the latter option to be able to negotiate a better deal.

The main benefit of owning a duplex is that you can get dual income right from the start and save quite a lot on land. Also, duplexes tend to be move-in ready or they require minimal renovation to make them more interesting for renters.

As for their versatility, you're only limited by your strategy. Some investors choose to live on one side and rent the other while others rent both sides, creating a stable cash flow and a positively-geared property.

Additionally, there are three options to finance a duplex – mortgage, owner-occupied loans, and owner-financing. And since we talked extensively about mortgages, I won't explain it here.

To get an owner-occupied loan, you'd need to live on one side, but it's still a good option for some first-time investors. As for owner-financing, I'd advise against this option because the equity builds too slowly and it's trickier to get it.

#4 – Townhouses

Townhouses usually have multiple levels, and they're designed to mimic stand-alone houses. However, unlike with stand-alone houses, you own only the strata title, meaning the land is shared with other people in your immediate neighbourhood. Some townhouses can be Torrens titled if they are a duplex.

The benefit is that these are often cheaper than stand-alone houses, but that may depend on the location. You may get more privacy than in an apartment. Nevertheless, townhouses come with a body corporate, so you'll have to deal with restrictions similar to owning an apartment.

However, if you have your eyes set on a really attractive location (a beachfront property, for example), a townhouse could be an outstanding deal. You may get highly desirable ocean views, stable rental income and yields, and decent capital growth.

That being said, you still need to be careful with your choice because the market shows that the capital growth for townhouses is closer to apartments rather than stand-alone houses or duplexes.

#5 – Commercial

Being the type of real estate that's designed for business purposes, commercial properties are generally stable investments with good capital gains potential. And there are a few types of commercial properties:

- Warehouses
- Offices/office buildings

- Industrial venues
- Retail
- Mixed-use building

Now, each type is specific in its own right and they're managed differently. And there are financial implications on commercial properties that are somewhat different compared to other property types. Plus, different taxation systems and property laws apply to this property type.

For example, commercial properties are subject to the services and goods taxes, which you have to pay upon purchase. That, plus some other expenses, add about 10% on top of the purchase price, assuming the property is vacant.

Speaking of vacancies, commercial properties can have very long untenanted periods, which affects their capital growth. And they're susceptible to changing economic factors such as unemployment rates, higher interest rates, market crashes, etc.

You need more capital upfront to purchase a commercial property, and lenders are stricter in terms of mortgage requirements. Generally, banks view commercial properties as riskier investments, which may result in:

- Higher deposits (often twice the amount you'd pay for a stand-alone house, for example)
- More scrutiny during the mortgage approval process
- Higher interest rates

Due to that, this property type is best suited for experienced investors who have sufficient expertise, time, and money.

What Property Type Did You Choose?

When all is said and done, stand-alone houses are the best option for first-time investors looking to grow their portfolios and achieve financial freedom in the long run.

Why?

First of all, you don't need to deal with the challenges of strata investments – the investor owns both the house and the land. And that may leave some room for subdivisions to further boost the returns on your investment.

Don't forget stand-alone houses are the most stable in terms of capital growth and rent increases. Plus, the lenders won't make you go above and beyond to get your mortgage approved.

However, duplexes could be a lucrative investment despite potential downsides. This is because they have the potential to provide you with an almost instant cash flow.

The next chapter explores creative strategies where you could use these property types to scale your portfolio.

CHAPTER 10

Creative Strategies

The previous chapter opened with a client story about a medical practitioner who had a lot of money to get in on the game.

But what if you're working with a tight budget?

Does that mean you can't get excellent capital growth and yields?

Of course not!

And the client I'd like to feature in this chapter attests to that.

They were a young couple with meagre combined super savings of only $200,000. Knowing they needed to boost their savings and improve finances, the couple decided property investment was the best way to go.

They set up an SMSF to invest in property with high capital growth potential, which further affirmed the creative strategy to be put to action.

We found a low-budget duplex that's cash flow-positive and had immense capital growth potential. In fact, it was in the top 10 Terry Rider growth areas for the next ten years.

The location was in NSW, just five minutes away from the nearest hospital and about half an hour from Newcastle and the local airport. Even better, the property was an hour's drive from Sydney.

But there was a massive depreciation in the area, giving us the upper hand during the negotiation process. And therefore, we got excellent results at the time of their purchase.

The asking price was $430,000, and we managed to drive that down to $420,000, saving the client $10,000. The LVR on the property is 70%, with a weekly rental income of $475, plus the vacancy rate was 1.8%.

After one year, the duplex got valued at $475,000, providing a capital growth of 13% or $55,000.

So, understanding how to be creative with your investments provides excellent yields. And, with a bit of help, it shouldn't be too hard for you to apply a similar strategy.

The Strategies

Duplexes aren't the only property type where you can be creative. The sections below will also explore renovations, splitter blocks, infill sites, and more.

#1 – Renovations

With renovations, the goal is to do it as cheaply as possible without hurting the property's capital growth potential. Consequently, you'll be able to maximise the profit on that particular real estate.

However, doing that isn't as easy as it may sound, and you shouldn't view renovation projects as a quick flip.

To do it the right way, you should employ the BRRRR strategy, which stands for Buy, Renovate, Rent, Refinance, and Repeat.

The first step with renovation is understanding the financial structure, location, and requirements. You need to know exactly how much money you need to borrow to cover the purchase and renovation.

Knowing that, you have to figure out the returns on the property after the renovation and how much capital gains you're looking to get.

But don't worry, renovated properties aren't usually vacant for too long, the rental returns are higher, and you're effectively engineering capital growth.

Still, you need to be extra careful when choosing the location. Some market studies show that around 80% of investment success boils down to the location.

Because of that, it's wise to work with buyer's and real estate agents and property consultants. As mentioned in Chapter 7, these professionals will help you pinpoint just the right property at the right time. More critically, they'll guide you through the negotiation to get the best price.

And it also pays to work with a property inspector to ensure the real estate doesn't require extensive renovations that would kill your profit.

#2 – Splitter Blocks

Also known as golden blocks, splitter blocks are property titles with two lots. This means the subdivision has already been done, saving you a lot of stress, money, and paperwork. Due to that, splitter blocks are among the most attractive investments.

To help you understand just how much you'd be saving, let's consider what happens when you want to subdivide a property.

In the process, you have to cover the council contribution fees, which are like a levy or tax. For instance, Brisbane requires you to pay almost $30,000 for each lot you create on the property.

Another benefit is that the Australian government exempts splitter blocks from minimum size lot regulations. But this isn't the case with subdivisions.

Plus, some studies show that 81% of larger splitter blocks (800sqm and larger) are in the hands of owners-occupiers. That indicates that there could be many opportunities to get one, especially if you look at properties that aren't listed in the market.

However, this percentage may vary based on the location you choose.

#3 – Infill Sites

Imagine this: you focus on an area that has been fully developed. The only thing left are small lots suitable for a specific type of vertical construction.

Now, I understand that this may sound like a significant challenge. And in many ways, it is. After all, you'll be embarking on a development project. But this doesn't mean there's no money to be made.

With the changing demographics, micro-apartments are becoming increasingly popular in some urban areas. And infill site developments are often viewed as socially responsible and sustainable construction.

However, not all infill sites are suitable for mid-rise buildings, for example. It depends on municipal regulation, zoning, and there's a possibility you'd need to consult with community or neighbourhood groups.

The silver lining is that you can resort to the Sustainable Development Code when negotiating with those in charge. The idea is that if you build a good property on a vacant lot, you'll be revitalising the neighbourhood. Plus, the new development helps against blight on that particular lot.

As for the property types suitable for infill lots, these include:

- High-rise parking
- Multi-family housing
- Mixed-use building (commercial + residential)

All in all, infill sites are attractive, but whether you should invest in one depends on your budget, size of the project, and access to infrastructure.

For instance, it's often easier to develop an infill site in an area with stand-alone houses. There won't be too much friction from the neighbourhood, and the infrastructure is often close by.

However, the logistics of developing an infill site in an urban area could turn into a nightmare. You may face neighbourhood restrictions, physical obstructions, community planning, and many more.

#4 – Subdivide

In the splitter blocks section, I mentioned that subdivisions could cost a pretty penny, especially if you want to add more than one lot.

But if you remember the client story from Chapter 9, you'll know there's great potential in subdivisions. As a quick reminder, the client renovated the existing house and subdivided the property to get two additional lots, earning more than $300,000 in eight months.

Anyway, when you want to do a subdivision, your plans need to be approved by the local council. So, you first need to consult with them to understand the criteria and requirements.

Thereon, you need to involve DAC (Development Assessment Commission) and a few professionals, such as private town planners, engineers, etc. The job of all these professionals is to complete the plans and submit them to the local council for approval.

Next, you'll need to prepare and submit many documents to the Land Titles Office, and a property lawyer can help you with that. The property lawyer will also assist you with the legal implications of subdividing the land.

But once you pull it off, you're looking at a much greater property flexibility and profits. You'll have more assets at your disposal to get super creative with your strategy.

For instance, you could develop the new lots, then sell one to get more cash for future investments.

#5 – Commercial

In Chapter 9, we discussed some of the challenges of investing in commercial real estate. And the COVID-19 pandemic has undoubtedly brought this segment of the market to a standstill.

However, we should revisit the topic and consider some potential benefits of investing in this property type.

For one, they are an excellent option to diversify your portfolio when you already have a few rental/residential properties. Of course, this goes if you invest in a cash flow-positive commercial property.

If the market springs back to life, you can expect pretty stable returns and income. Also, commercial properties may allow for greater investment control and more options to add value. The rental yields are higher, and tenants usually pay all the outgoings.

On top of that, you may gain a higher capacity to leverage against a commercial property to further grow your portfolio.

Though, you shouldn't forget that commercial properties are complex to finance and run. And there are unique leasing arrangements that may involve a team of lawyers.

But the leases are usually long-term, giving you the benefit of stable, predictable cash flow.

Get Your Creative Juices Flowing

Lastly, choosing the right creative strategy should be based on your investment goals, budget, and current property portfolio.

If you're a first-time investor, it's best to go for a duplex, as the couple mentioned at the beginning of the chapter. Splitter blocks are also a great option since they require much less legwork than subdivisions, for example.

However, those who already have a few cash flow-positive properties may want to venture into infill sites or commercial properties.

But whichever strategy you choose, it's vital to do your homework and understand all the intricacies of the projects. Otherwise, you could grossly underestimate the budget, timeframe, and legal requirements.

That could hurt your profit or even negatively gear the property. To that end, the money you spend on consulting with experts is money well spent.

Why?

You probably won't have the time or nerves to do all the research and paperwork yourself. Even worse, you may lose motivation to invest in the first place. Mitigating risk in property investing will make the difference as you build your property portfolio for a good retirement.

CHAPTER 11

Using Equity to Grow Your Property Portfolio

This client of mine decided to go with a joint venture (JV) deal which included a triplex development and strata.

But like most of my clients, he's a busy young professional who didn't have the time to do the research. Also, he couldn't embark on a development project of that scale on his own.

However, the guy understood the power of property investments to grow his wealth. So, he became a part of the *I Love Real Estate* community.

More importantly, he was eager to share his skills and knowledge as a carpenter.

But the critical thing was that he needed to keep working full time and earn money through his trade. Therefore, he needed to find the right strategy and partner to pull it all off.

Now, what kind of a deal did we find for this carpenter-turned-investor?

The right property came up in Launceston, Tasmania. There was an existing house with a lot of intrinsic value and 1,010sqm of land with an option to subdivide and build two villas at the back of the property.

Plus, it all came with a strata title and battle-axe access in the CBD.

Note that the whole deal was cash flow positive, and we decided to renovate and then rent the existing house while the two additional villas were being developed.

When the two extra properties were completed, everything would be sold off for a profit.

But how much profit did this client actually earn?

After selling everything and covering the expenses, the profit was a whopping $220,000. This was about a 22% return after covering all the expenses. But keep in mind that the client needed to split it 40/60 with his partner.

Anyway, the house and the land cost $365,000 and the renovation and construction added another $615,000, putting the grand total at $980,000.

All the properties were sold for 1.2 million, leaving more than enough money for both partners in this deal.

The Equity You Could Get From a Duplex

Yes, the example above covers the equity from a triplex, but this doesn't mean you can't do well on a duplex. With that in mind, there are certain things to consider if you want to take full advantage of your property portfolio.

Understand the Numbers

You should know that some of the equity in your portfolio is unusable.

Why?

The banks usually lend you about 80% of a property value, and you need to deduct the money you owe from that. To bring the numbers closer to you, let's say you want to get an $850,000 property.

So, your property is $850,000, the bank covers $680,000 (80%), and you're left with $170,000 in equity. And you can put that money towards your next investment.

Of course, as your property becomes more valuable, your equity increases with it. And you should also know that lenders may cover about 95% of the equity.

However, you can get 95% funding only if you cover the LMI (Lenders Mortgage Insurance) on the amount that exceeds 80% of the investment.

That safeguards the bank if you default, and it's an additional expense that eats into your equity.

Also, when calculating usable equity, you need to know exactly how much you'll be spending on the investment. And, on that note, we come to our next point.

Budgeting

Some investors breathe a sigh of relief when there's high capital growth in their portfolios.

Great!

But you still need to be frugal about your budget and constantly re-evaluate your capacity to repay loans before venturing into another investment.

This applies even if you find a great property under the market value. That real estate could be a bargain, but you'll still need to cover all the expenses and be liquid enough to get your mortgage approved.

Be aware that lenders usually have a stringent vetting procedure and may turn you down despite having equity in your portfolio.

The reason being that few banks would be willing to approve a loan based on equity alone. Instead, they'd consider the following:

- Age
- Expenses
- Income
- Your dependants

And if any of the given criteria indicates that you're close to being overdrawn, the bank may refuse to loan you money.

Other than that, you need to ensure your finance isn't stretched too far. Usually, this means that you can cover the mortgage and maintenance on an untenanted duplex for at least a few months. Also, you shouldn't forget about strata and insurance levies, management fees (if applicable).

Therefore, it would be wise to consult with your accountant or financial advisor to determine how much equity you can actually use. Always keep in mind that there should be some money left to cover unexpected expenses or the cost of a vacant property.

Max Out the Equity

You need to be proactive and consider ways to maximise the equity even before you buy the duplex.

Repaying the mortgage in advance is one way to do it. And there's always the option to wait until the prices rise and leverage that capital gain.

But before you buy the property, focus on finding the perfect location because it's one of the keys to growing equity fast.

As mentioned before, the idea is to find a location with excellent capital growth potential. These are the areas with zoning changes on the horizon or those with pending infrastructure projects.

And if you renovate, you'll add value to the property even sooner than that. But it's critical to be careful not to stretch your budget too far. If the value increases just by the amount you invested in the renovation, you aren't adding equity. At least, not in the short term.

That being said, duplexes are fantastic because you have more room to maximise the equity because you're going to renovate.

Take the example from the beginning of this chapter. The property itself was just shy of $400,000, but the renovation and development added another $600,000. And it was vital that the investors knew these numbers before they started.

In Equity We Trust

Equity gives you the power to purchase a property every year and sustainably grow your portfolio.

But it's critical to be careful with your finance and property selection. You want to ensure you have enough cash to cover all the related expenses and still have some money left.

But if you keep purchasing positively-geared properties, that shouldn't be too much of a problem. Additionally, some property types like duplexes allow you to have a flexible exit strategy.

This means that you'll be able to cover a large chunk of your debt by selling one unit in a duplex, for example. Then, allocate that money towards another property.

CHAPTER 12

The Strategy – Ten Properties in Ten Years

In the previous chapter, we talked about understanding equity and how it helps build a bulletproof portfolio.

Here, we'll continue discussing duplexes as one of the best property types to ensure you have ten properties in ten years.

But before we do that, it pays to cover another client story to show you that it's possible to get into real estate investments with any kind of budget.

These clients were a newly married couple and had very little understanding of how to get in on the property game. However, they knew real estate is the best way to grow their wealth and get some additional cash.

Anyway, this couple wanted a house with some land where they could build in the future. The idea was to venture into a low-cost property where they could subdivide, then build or sell the land depending on their financial plans.

But what was the strategy?

We were looking for a cash flow-positive property with good capital growth potential. And sure, it had to feature a development opportunity.

The property that fitted the bill appeared in Tasmania. There was an existing house, 825sqm of land, and it was all about 400m from the neighbouring lake.

But the best thing was that the seller asked for $300,000 for the whole lot. This didn't stretch the couple's budget and they got the property for that price.

On top of that, the weekly rental return for the house was $320. And the rental yield was 5.5% in an area with a vacancy rate of 0.95%. So, the couple didn't really have to worry about getting tenants, even though the competition was a bit tight.

The deal itself worked great and they are now renting the property and have enough cash to cover all the expenses.

At the time of writing, the couple was still raising money to subdivide the land and build another house there.

When that happens, the couple will likely cover the mortgage for the first house and still have the rental income. So, they'll have a debt-free property to play around with and further grow their portfolio.

Getting the 10 Properties

Yes, duplexes are a great way to get a ten-property portfolio in ten years. The strategy appears straightforward, develop or renovate a duplex, and sell one unit and keep the other. Then, repeat the process every year.

However, the strategy to grow your portfolio with duplexes is more nuanced than that. You need to know how to prepare and mitigate risk as much as possible.

The following sections explore the critical criteria to consider before venturing into a duplex.

The Reasons to Invest

Think about what you wish to do with the property once it's done. This is the first step that helps you gauge if it's feasible and how much money you need to complete it.

As mentioned in the previous chapter, there are several options:

- Selling both units
- Sell one, rent one (this is the strategy you should be aiming for)
- Rent both units
- Live in one unit, and rent or sell the other

The last option is also a great way to start growing your portfolio because it's possible to live in one unit almost expense free.

But if you're developing a duplex from the ground up, it's not only a matter of choosing the appropriate rent or sell strategy.

Duplexes are an excellent property type to build capital growth without waiting years for it to happen. But the construction itself might take up to 12 months, and you need to be sure it won't be too much of a strain on your finances.

Be that as it may, you can take some equity from a duplex as soon as it's finished. And that money will allow you to immediately venture into another real estate deal.

Plus, you have the benefit of dual income but paid for only one lot or subdivision.

To understand the actual numbers, take Gold Coast in Queensland, for example.

A three-bedroom stand-alone house in Palm Beach rents at about $650 a week. Just a few streets down that neighbourhood, there are identical size duplexes that rent for $550 for each unit.

The maths is simple. Investors get $450 more for a duplex in basically the same area.

Location, Location, Location

In Chapter 11, we touched on the importance of location. But since the location can make or break your investments, it pays to revisit the topic.

First of all, it's best to buy or develop in a familiar area. If that's not possible, you should be looking for a location that ticks all the right boxes in terms of growth:

- Proximity to cities, employment hubs, etc.
- Good infrastructure, or the potential to extend the infrastructure

- Stable population growth
- Good rental demand
- The proximity of entertainment venues, schools, and shopping centres

And there's another factor to keep in mind. You need to be diligent and inspect the current zoning and future rezoning, if applicable.

The thing is that municipal regulations may vary, and you need to keep checking them to ensure you're in line with the law. Note that two lots just a couple of streets away might not be subject to the same regulations.

Also, if you want to develop a duplex, it's best to get a feasibility study. This appears like an unnecessary step, but it can save you a lot of headaches in the long run.

A feasibility study clearly shows you if you're in the money or not. It takes all the related expenses, starting with the purchase price and moving on to the taxes and fees after you sell.

Then, when you subtract from the expected sales price, you'll know if you're in the profit or not.

But all that goes under the pretence that there won't be any downward trends until your duplex is finished.

Choosing a Builder

Of course, this section applies to those who wish to develop a duplex. But even if you don't, it won't hurt to know what makes a great builder.

A reputable builder often has a display duplex or home. Check that to inspect the level of quality and craftsmanship you could get in your development.

These builders could be up to 20% more expensive than the competition, but you're getting peace of mind that everything will be done just as you want it.

However, it's also okay to go with subcontractors who work with big reputable builders. They're great if you're on a tight budget and want high-level service and construction.

At best, the company you work with will have a draftsperson or an in-house architect. But you shouldn't assume that these professionals know all the zoning regulations for the site you purchased.

Finally, if you're unsure which builder to choose, we're here to help you find the one that can provide a turnkey solution just in time for you to make a profit.

The Positive and Negative Sides of Investing in Duplexes

We've already covered some of the upsides, such as having a dual income and different exit strategies. But the story doesn't end there, and there are certain downsides you should know about.

To start with the good, a positively-geared duplex allows you to be tactical in building your equity. Simply put, you have the option to engineer how to maximise your returns and profit.

Due to that, duplexes are great for first-time investors who don't have the time and knowledge to deal with all the nuances of a real estate evaluation.

Since duplexes allow you to grow your portfolio each year, they are a good option for retirees or those who are about to retire.

They might not aim for ten properties in ten years. But duplexes certainly allow them to boost their wealth and potentially supplement their super.

Also, duplexes are a hot commodity, so you won't struggle to find tenants or buyers. There are plenty of experts specialising in this niche, and you can find all the help you need to make it happen.

So far so good, but what about the negative aspects?

Duplexes are a high yield and growth investment. That's great, but it means that it needs more financial commitment on your side.

If you want to get a duplex rather than develop one, know that the price usually reflects the property's condition. Getting something just because it's inexpensive usually means you'll end up with a dud that's not worth your time and money.

Also, those who wish to build need to put down a 20% deposit. In a previous chapter, we discussed an option to get a lower deposit, but you don't want that because it increases risk.

To touch upon location again, some councils forbid duplex construction. But we're here to help you find the right location, so you shouldn't worry too much about the council regulations.

Build Your Portfolio One Duplex at a Time

Getting ten properties in ten years doesn't sound like a far-fetched goal.

You get one duplex, sell one unit, keep the other, and repeat the process until you hit that goal. Even better, you now know all the challenges of buying or developing a duplex, so it should be much easier to choose the right strategy.

But those ten properties aren't there to only build your wealth. They can secure a retirement most people dream about, and that's what we'll discuss in the next chapter.

To give you a hint, the idea is to secure a stable cash flow that might even make you forget about your super.

CHAPTER 13

Using Property as Your Retirement Vehicle

Imagine this – you come to retirement age, and there are ten or more properties in your portfolio.

Not only that, but these properties are also debt-free and have accumulated so much capital growth that you don't have to worry about money at all.

Understandably, some of you might not think that far ahead, but it's never too early to start planning for your retirement.

To show you how you can use properties as a retirement vehicle, let's discuss a family duo that utilised their property investment to grow their super.

So this is a mother-daughter team, and they had some knowledge of property investments. However, they needed some external help to pull it all off without making any costly mistakes.

The strategy was – the mother and daughter put the money together and set up an SMSF, which would allow them to invest.

Like always, we were looking for a cash flow-positive property with good yields and capital growth.

One such property appeared in NSW, and they jumped at the opportunity. It was a dual occupancy in a growth area with lots of gentrification.

Better yet, the property was near the local schools, a freeway, and a hospital.

This may lead you to believe that our duo had to pay a pretty penny to get the property. But you'd be wrong because we managed to significantly drive down the price.

The seller was asking for $350,000. After some negotiation, we settled on $335,000, saving them $15,000 right from the get-go.

The rental income for that entire property was $500 per week, with a tremendous annual rental return of about 8%. Plus, it's in the area with a 0.9% vacancy rate.

The mother and daughter could pick and choose their tenants and not worry if the property sat on the market for too long.

But the beauty of this deal is that the value and yields are only going to grow. Since the location is so attractive, our investors are looking at some great returns by the time they need to retire.

Anyway, the following section will cover specific aspects of the current retirement crisis. And you'll get actionable tips and insights on how to take full advantage of your investment to secure a comfortable retirement.

Explaining the Australian Retirement Crisis

The truth is that Australian seniors need about $72,000 per year per person to enjoy a comfortable retirement.

Some predictions state that super will provide between 5% and 7% returns a year. But this still doesn't give you a clear picture of how much money you'll need.

And yes, $72,000 a year doesn't sound too bad, but securing that money is an entirely different ballgame.

For example, take the baby boomers who are of retirement age right now. Their main concern is to calculate their exact cost of living. Then, they need to figure out if their super is going to be enough to cover all the expenses.

Most likely, it's not, and they'd need to find a solution to supplement or grow their super.

With that in mind, the Australian retirement crisis is yet to hit seniors in its full swing. But that's all the more reason to be tactical and proactive.

Now, the Australian net worth was $410,708 per capita in 2018. That put Australians among the ten best countries in the world, and the rise in property value largely contributed to that.

On the surface, everything may appear fine, until you start digging a bit deeper.

According to the data from 2017 to 2018, more than 70% of households had a sizeable debt. Even more alarming, about 30% of the homes had to cover mortgages that exceeded disposable income threefold.

Then there's the wealth distribution. The saddening truth is that Australian ten percenters hold close to 50% of the available assets. And the same goes for savings.

Knowing all that, the average super of $270,710 for men and $157,050 for women appear meagre compared to how much they need.

So how much is it, exactly?

Getting the answer to this question is tricky because it's not like one number fits all. The aforementioned $72,000 a year is a good ballpark figure, but there are different factors one needs to consider.

First and foremost, a person's lifestyle and current financial standing. Other than that, retirees need to consider if they own a rental property or not.

Also, sizeable savings that could be put towards property investments help. And ideally, they'd get a material inheritance they can leverage to grow their super.

If all goes well and they save, then reinvest a lot, boomers could be looking forward towards a comfortable retirement.

But why wait and speculate when strategic property investments can take the edge off your finances in senior years?

Can Property Provide a Good Return for Retirement?

The quick answer is yes, it can. But to understand the financial mechanism behind that, it pays to dig a bit deeper.

To begin with, property investments provide you with security. And this isn't only about whether you're going to earn money or not. Instead, security refers to the fact that the value and capital gains of your property will enable you to have a financially stable retirement.

Sure, not all property investments are the same, and some areas are just more lucrative than others. But by now, you should have a complete understanding of where to look and what kind of property to get.

Also, specific predictions are favourable when it comes to property price growth, particularly in the coming years.

That out of the way, you should remember that properties can provide stable income and cash flow through rent or sales. This income will work great towards getting your super to a comfortable level.

Of course, your super income may stay intact while you can use the property income to support yourself.

On top of that, property investments boost your long-term liquidity. This means you'll have a higher capacity to access capital whenever you need it. And with property, you can access that capital at any time.

Should you find yourself in a difficult situation, there's always an option to sell one or more properties to secure the money you need.

To access your super, you need to be 65 and retired. You can also access the funds through TRP (Transitional Retirement Pensions), but there's a cap on the amount you can take out.

With that in mind, it's hard to access capital from the property until you sell it off. But this is why we always look for duplexes, subdivisions, and other property types that allow for different exit strategies.

Anyway, you also need to think about capital growth, inflation, and the flexibility of your investment.

As for capital growth, you already know it's stable with property investments in the long run. However, your super might not yield such significant returns that could cover your cost of living in old age. But there's a way to merge the best of both worlds and grow your portfolio within the super.

Inflation-wise, properties work great towards offsetting the inflation increases. Even if there's another GFC (Global Financial Crisis), properties will still perform well. But it's not like that with assets such as fixed savings, interest, or cash.

Finally, properties are among the most flexible investments you can get. That means you'll be able to change the strategy or the asset itself during its lifecycle.

This ties back to some of the benefits of duplexes, for example. Since you can use different strategies to get a stable cash flow from a duplex, that's a flexible investment.

But don't forget that you can change investment options within a super fund as well. This is usually with the assets that are held within the fund.

Seven Property Techniques You Can Use to Make Property Your Retirement Vehicle

#1 – Cash Flow-Positive Properties

As mentioned before, a cash flow-positive property brings in some instant money. Renting a property as soon as you get it should be enough to cover the expenses and still have some money left.

And since you're aiming to invest more and grow your portfolio, you'll find a property with potential for rental increases and capital growth. Then, you'll be able to leverage that to buy more and get yourself the lifestyle you deserve.

But what if the rent remains stagnant for a long period?

That almost never happens! And if it does, it may affect the capital growth on a particular property.

Even so, stagnant rent isn't necessarily going to hurt your capacity to purchase more positively-geared properties.

#2 – Buy and Hold (Income vs Capital Gains)

There are two buy and hold strategies.

One is to purchase a negatively-geared property and wait for the rental income to increase so that it can cover all the expenses and mortgage. However, I've already explained how flawed this strategy is.

The other option is to buy a positively-geared property, then hold it until there are enough capital gains to live from the equity alone. Or you could borrow money against that equity to reinvest or cover the gap between your income and expenses.

But the second strategy may take up to 10 years to yield results. Also, you might rely on borrowing to cover expenses and the cost of living. The latter goes unless you keep reinvesting in properties.

#3 – Renovations

There could be a lot of hidden value in a property that needs a bit of TLC, assuming you get it for a bargain in a very attractive location. The key thing with renovations is to ensure you don't overspend and hurt your returns.

Also, it's critical to set a clear deadline on when the job needs to get done. If it takes months upon months to finish up a renovation, you'll be losing potential income. In addition, the costs might substantially exceed your budget.

#4 – *Vendor Financing*

Vendor financing is a specific strategy where you don't sell a property for cash.

Instead, this set-up is like a transfer of your mortgage to the property buyer. Now, you might believe this isn't an ideal thing to do, but there are certain benefits.

The buyer will agree to pay well above the market price, so you're in the money right away. Plus, the buyer also pays a higher interest rate, putting even more money in your pocket.

The term for vendor financing is 25 years, but you can expect the buyer to pay in full much sooner than that.

#5 – *Commercial*

Throughout this book, we touched upon commercial properties and how lucrative an investment they can be.

To remind you, this property type requires a higher down payment (usually about 30%). Also, commercial properties offer higher rental income. And the rental period is much longer as businesses aren't likely to move as frequently as regular tenants.

However, vacant commercial properties may sit on the market for a long time before they're occupied. Therefore, you need to have a stable cash flow to cover all the expenses while the property is untenanted.

More critically, note that the demand for commercial properties might not be that high because of COVID.

#6 – Super as Investment Vehicle

SMSFs (Self-Managed Super Funds) give you the option to manage the super yourself.

In other words, you can access the money and invest. Additionally, SMSF allows you to borrow against an investment property.

There are tax benefits, so SMSF has become a popular tactic to grow one's portfolio fast.

#7 – Maxing Out the Leverage

If you max out the leverage, you'll be able to get more properties because there's less money to deposit.

To do that, you need LMI (Lenders Mortgage Insurance). As mentioned in one of the previous chapters, LMI is there to mitigate the lender's risk.

This strategy is good when you want to quickly grow your portfolio, but it could be very risky for the long haul.

The reason is that if the property value drops and interest rates increase, you might struggle to cover the expenses. And since the bank won't be willing to wait it out, they could push you to sell the property to cover the debt.

Carefree Retirement

When all is said and done, it's safe to say that property investments are one of the best ways to secure a financially stable retirement. Plus, it's an excellent option to supplement your super or savings.

Given the yield and capital gains from real estate, you'll be getting much higher returns on your money. Not only that, but you'll also accumulate hard debt-free assets.

As a result, you'll have the benefit of more flexible exit plans when you want to retire. You could sell everything off and live off the profit. Or you might want to keep some of your high rental yield properties to have a stable recurring cash flow.

But whatever you choose, properties will allow you to live through your senior years just like you wanted.

CHAPTER 14

Positive Cash Flow is King – How to Be Your Own Boss

I'd like to open this chapter with a story about a client who's a mortgage broker with a good business turnover.

When the client decided to go into property investments, the goal was to leverage the services of an experienced property developer and investor. Ultimately, this client wanted to gain instant equity and grow his property portfolio.

Therefore, the best way to go was to enter a joint venture.

But what was the investment strategy that we employed?

The optimal course of action was to find a suitable location and subdivide the land to allow for a large development. And the perfect place appeared at Lake Macquarie, LGA.

We found an old house on a large block of land overlooking the lake. The strategy was to demolish the old house, subdivide the land, then build six townhouses and sell them off.

Since this was a joint venture, the client shared the construction and acquisition costs with Msisa Property and Consulting Agents – an agency that provides the expertise and manages the project from acquisition to sales. And the two parties agreed on a 50/50 profit share.

Now, let's talk about the actual deal.

The land size was 1669sqm in an R2 zoning area. The initial asking price was $570,000, but the client offered $30,000 more because there were multiple bidders. And it's important to stress that this action didn't hurt the profitability.

When you add the construction and planning, the grand total was $2.9 million. But each townhouse sold for $650,000, making the client $1 million, or 34% gross realisation.

Of course, that was before the cost, and after the cost was subtracted, the profit was $700,000, or 24% net realisation. And each partner in the joint venture ended up with $350,000.

What Does Investing for Positive Cash Flow Mean?

To begin with, you need to understand what a cash flow-positive property is.

Simply put, this is a property that provides annual rent which is greater than the annual expenses. And yes, this is after the depreciation and tax deductions.

Also, you can regard this as a property that immediately offers an income. Plus, it doesn't strain the household income, assuming you'll be leveraging the property. But this is hardly the only advantage of owning such a property.

Another key benefit is that you can make even more money since the property is bound to appreciate as time goes by.

To highlight the point, it's best to give you an example so you understand how this kind of deal works in real life.

The Example

Let's say you get a property for around $500,000, and it provides $24,000 in yearly rental income.

Now, assume that the yearly loan interest amounts to about $23,000. Add a few thousand in related expenses and it becomes evident that this appears to be a negatively-geared property.

However, this is before the taxes and deductions you'll be able to claim.

For example, the depreciation for fittings and building and the loan costs are the non-cash deductions you can claim. And for a $500,000 property, these may exceed $7,000 in the first year.

Here, I'd like to take a slight detour and explain the non-cash deductions in general. These are the deductions you're eligible to claim, but you don't need to spend any cash out of pocket to fund the related expenses.

Back to the story – what happens after tax and deductions?

First of all, you should know that you may be able to report on-paper losses that exceed $10,000 in the first year. That allows you to claim more than $4,000 tax back, given the amount of on-paper losses.

After all the deductions, taxes, and expenses, this kind of property gives you about $1,000 of positive cash flow in the first year.

Sure, I know it's not much, but your cash flow will increase over time.

In the second year, it'll be more than $1,600, in the fourth year more than $1,800, and so on. Again, this doesn't look like something that will make you a millionaire, but keep one thing in mind…

These are the numbers after all the expenses and taxes get covered. On top of that, your property will appreciate, putting even more money in your pockets.

The Benefits of Investing in Positive Cash Flow

#1 – You'll Make Money From Day One

With positively-geared properties, the money you get from rent is enough to cover all your expenses, mortgage included.

Keep in mind that things like stamp duty, solicitor fees, and maintenance costs add up fast. So, with negatively-geared properties, you need to cover all that out of pocket and wait for the properties to increase in value to start getting some returns.

But most novice investors don't have the time or funds to finance negatively-geared properties. And the tax breaks they get might not be enough to make up all that's lost.

#2 – *Positive Cash Flow Properties Pay for Themselves*

Since you're getting money to cover all your expenses, financing cash flow-positive properties won't strain your budget.

The income pays for your debt and maintenance on the property, and you may even have some money left to reinvest or upgrade your property for better rental returns.

Also, some investors use interest-only loans until they get a bigger cash flow. Then, they switch to interest and principal loan when they secure the stable cash flow of a long-term lease, for example.

Note that the strategy above is something you'd need to discuss with your lender as it might not be available to all investors.

#3 – *Safeguarding Your Income and Property Portfolio*

We all know that businesses and markets can take a turn for the worse.

But with the extra cash you're getting from positively-geared properties, you can offset the financial impact. Imagine you have five positively-geared properties where two of those lose tenants or need costly repairs.

In that case, you can use the money that's coming in from the remaining properties to cover related expenses. And the great thing is that you won't feel the financial strain. These properties are probably generating more than enough to keep your portfolio stable.

But if the same happened with negatively-geared property, you might need to sell one of them to avoid losing a substantial amount of cash.

#4 – *You Don't Limit Your Borrowing Capacity*

Generally, it's hard to borrow money against a negatively-geared property. So, you won't be able to grow your portfolio at a stable pace.

But, since positive cash flow properties pay for themselves and offer good capital growth, you shouldn't struggle to find a lender willing to lend against them. Since your property will be earning money right from the start, that makes the mortgage safer in the eyes of lenders.

That being said, mortgage criteria aren't fixed, so you may want to consult with your mortgage broker to determine how much you can actually borrow. But still, there won't be a major cap on your ability to grow the portfolio.

Four Tips for Finding Positive Cash Flow Properties

#1 – *Calculations*

When you find a promising property, you need to do the maths to determine if it's cash flow positive or not. But there's a common trap you should avoid because the calculation isn't as simple as it seems.

For instance, your weekly mortgage and rental income may lead you to believe that the property is neutral. However, it doesn't factor in other expenses that could put you in the red. And these may vary widely depending on the property you get.

At best, you should learn how to calculate a property's cash flow even before you start looking for one. I can help you with that. The general idea is to set the potential income against all the expenses, including insurance, maintenance, council rates, etc.

#2 – Using Free Resources

You don't need to pay a small fortune just to find a great property. There are a bunch of websites that offer comprehensive property information for free.

Better yet, these websites often provide potential rental returns, giving you the upper hand to calculate the cash flow.

And if you don't trust that, you can always get in touch with a real estate agent. They'll be willing to estimate rental income for you since you're a serious investor.

But of course, using the free resources is only the first step. Next, you need to know how to analyse the information to gauge if a property is good from an investment standpoint. Just to clarify, I'm referring to long-term capital gains here.

#3 – Rural and Mining Towns

Take Tamworth and Dubbo in NSW. They are great examples of promising towns.

Why?

First of all, these are bigger town centres, not cities. Therefore, you're likely to pay a fraction of the price compared to Melbourne and Sydney.

That being said, you shouldn't assume that finding a cash flow-positive deal in mining and rural towns is easier. You still need to do your due diligence and analyse the property.

But if you do it right, you could be looking at a much higher cash flow compared to the big cities. And I should stress that all of the above goes only if the rental demand is high. Otherwise, you'd struggle to make the deal work no matter how cheap the property might be.

#4 – Dual Occupancies and Granny Flats

Be it in cities or rural areas, dual occupancies are a great way to get a high cash flow. These are properties that have two separate living areas. Each should feature a bathroom, kitchen, and all the other amenities.

As for the granny flats, these could be promising development projects, particularly in bigger cities.

Why?

The demand for granny flats is on the rise. Because of that, the local government in cities like Sydney has made it straightforward to get approval for such a development.

Focus on the Positive

Getting a cash flow-positive property isn't as hard as it might seem. But still, there are specific criteria a property needs to meet.

As mentioned in the previous chapters, you need to find an area with a good rental yield and growth. And the property itself shouldn't be a money pit, even if you choose to renovate it.

However, the most important thing is to do all your calculations right. There are many properties that may appear great at first look. But once you dive into the expenses, it becomes clear there's no way to make money from them.

CHAPTER 15

Retire in Style – Investing Through a Self-Managed Super Fund

Imagine this – by the time you get to retirement age, you have more than enough money to lead the lifestyle you've always wanted.

I know that this may sound like a pipe dream, but it's possible to do it via investing through a self-managed super fund.

But you shouldn't take my word for it. I want you to carefully consider the client example I'll share here to determine just how much money you could be looking at.

This client of mine is a couple who decided to put their hard-earned money together and invest in property for capital growth.

They both work as nurses and, like many of my clients, their knowledge of property investments was limited. Nevertheless, the couple understood it was the best way to go if they were to secure a fulfilled retirement for themselves.

Now, what was the strategy we employed to give them the desired returns?

Like always, we set our eyes on a cash flow-positive property with good rental yields and great long-term capital growth. And it wasn't long before one such property appeared in NSW.

Sure, you're wondering about the numbers.

The property's asking price was $450,000 and, after some negotiation, we managed to drive the price down to $425,000. Immediately, the client saved $25,000.

But when you account for the weekly rental income and the growth yield, things become even better.

The weekly rental income was $450, and the property yielded an amazing $55,000 just six months after the purchase. I mean, it was valued at $480,000, providing a 12% increase with a vacancy rate of 1.2%.

More importantly, all that happened despite the COVID pandemic. And it's safe to assume the property will yield even more after the pandemic is over.

I won't be going out on a limb to say that this particular property could more than double its price by the time the couple gets to retirement age.

With that in mind, there's no reason you couldn't do the same. The following sections give you all the necessary information about SMSFs and how to use them for property investments.

What Are SMSFs?

SMSF is an abbreviation of self-managed super fund. This is one of the methods to save up enough money for retirement, but there's one key difference compared to other funds.

With SMSFs, the members within the fund are trustees.

But what does being a trustee and a member mean?

It means the fund runs for the benefit of its members. They're accountable for all the legal proceedings, including tax and super law compliance.

Of course, the first action is to set up the fund correctly, and there are a few steps to that.

Start by soliciting some professional help to ensure no stones are left unturned. Then, determine if you want to appoint a corporate or individual trustees. Since you're a private investor, individual trustees would be the way to go.

After appointing the trustees, the next step is to create the trust itself and the trust deed. Thereon, register the fund, obtain an ABN, and create a bank account specific to that fund.

The final two steps are to obtain the electronic service address and develop the most favourable exit strategy for when it comes time to retire.

Note that the steps for setting up SMSF appear straightforward. But there are many nuances and legal requirements, so it's still best to ask for professional help.

As for investing through the fund, you need to do it according to the law and for the best interest of all the members (trustees). Also, it's critical to keep your other business affairs and personal finance separate from the funds.

To do that the right way, you need to create a property investment strategy that supports your long-term investment goals. Think carefully about how and why you should use the SMSF to achieve these.

And keep in mind that super laws require you to prepare the strategy, then implement it accordingly. Plus, you need to review the strategy's effectiveness regularly.

How to Invest in Property Using an SMSF

Sure, your strategy informs the type of property investments and how to use the fund. Even so, there are a few critical aspects to remember.

#1 – Residential Properties

Should you choose to invest in residential properties, keep in mind that you can't live in that property. The same goes for any other fund members and trustees. And it doesn't matter if you're in a distant relationship.

Additionally, you and other trustees won't be able to rent the property. To put it bluntly, you can't invest in a seaside property and move there for the summer. The law prohibits that.

Lastly, you can't cheat the law and add your existing property to the SMSF. This applies should you try to buy your property or make a financial contribution to it.

#2 – Commercial Properties

In general, SMSF commercial property investments are more advantageous compared to residential.

Why?

For one, you already know that getting a residential property forbids you from living there. You can't be the one who rents it. Critically, there's no way to add an existing property to an SMSF.

But commercial property is different.

SMSF members can sell commercial property to the fund. Also, the trustees are allowed to be the ones who lease that property, either as a business or an individual.

That sounds great, but you should note that there's a particular application to get an SMSF loan for commercial properties.

Usually, the vetting process is much stricter compared to residential properties. Therefore, this isn't something novice investors should consider.

#3 – Taxation Systems

When you invest in a property through SMSF, there's a 15% tax on the rental income. If the property stays within the fund for 12 months or more, there's a discount of a third on capital gains after-sales.

In other words, the capital gains tax shrinks to 10%.

Should you take out a loan to get the property, your interest payments are eligible for deductions. Also, if there are losses on the property, you can use them to offset taxable income in the future.

But the great thing happens when you retire. At that time, the capital gains and rental income within the fund are tax-free.

#4 – SMSF – Borrowing Criteria

As mentioned, the borrowing criteria for commercial properties are stringent. However, the same could be said for SMSF borrowing criteria in general.

Compared to what you may get from a bank, these loans cost more. And you need to factor that in when determining if your property will be cash flow positive or not.

At the time of writing, the consensus of financial institutions is that they'll only lend to a fund if it already has $200,000 or more.

To determine if you're eligible to borrow against the fund, make sure to consult with your bank or financial advisor.

This is critical because any mortgage payments will be made through the fund, not your personal or business account. Therefore, you need to be sure there's always enough money in the SMSF.

The Five Tips for Using an SMSF to Invest (and Ensure You Meet All Regulations)

#1 – Looking at Smaller Banks

In all honesty, the big banks are rarely willing to lend to SMSFs.

Why?

This type of borrowing is only about 0.18% of the entire market, so the numbers don't add up from the banks' perspective. And that's mainly because they need to do a lot of compliance to make the deal work.

Be that as it may, you'd want to look at smaller banks and other lenders who are willing to do their share of the work. Luckily, there are many such institutions.

As a rule, you'll be asked to put down a 20% deposit. But some lenders may ask for up to 30%. And you could be paying higher interest than what you'd get with a loan outside an SMSF.

#2 – *Investing Early*

Back in 2014, the Murray Report analysed the housing affordability in the country. Alarmingly, the report suggested creating a strategy to limit the super funds and investor activity.

If the authorities adopt a strategy that would cap your investment capacity, the plan to invest through SMSF is at risk. Worse yet, you might not be able to invest at all.

The silver lining is that none of the proposed restrictions came through. But there's still a possibility that the government might change course in the future.

To protect yourself from abrupt regulation changes, it's best to start investing through your SMSF as early as possible.

#3 – *Knowing the Restrictions*

SMSFs allow you to invest in residential, commercial, and even industrial properties. But there are specific rules and regulations to follow.

You already know that you can't live in the residential property or be the one who rents it. And the same applies to entities related to the trustees within the SMSF.

Also, you can't buy a property from your family members or any other related party. Then, there's the "sole purpose" rule, which means the only purpose of your investment is the retirement benefits.

It's critical to follow these rules to the T to avoid jeopardising the future of your investments.

#4 – Renovation Rules

There's an assumption that you can't renovate a property using your SMSF. But this isn't entirely true.

Indeed, you can renovate as long as you follow specific rules.

It's possible to use SMSF funds to upgrade your property and add value to it. However, you can't use borrowed money to do that.

For instance, you can't take out a personal loan to upgrade the plumbing. The money needs to be taken out from the SMSF.

That being said, there are some instances where you can use the borrowed money – maintenance costs, for example.

#5 – Limited Resources Borrowing

The first option to get a property through SMSF is to purchase one using the money from the fund. However, if you haven't saved up enough, you'd need to create an LRBA (Limited Resource Borrowing Arrangement).

So, what's that?

The arrangement represents a set of borrowing conditions that allow you to get a property. With LRBA, you can only get one asset, whether commercial or residential, but there's a silver lining.

The conditions of the arrangement protect you should the investment fail. The lenders are allowed to only claim the money lost in the property deal. That is, they can't access the funds in your super.

Make a Super Comfortable Retirement

Without a doubt, using your SMSF to start investing in prosperity is one of the best ways to secure a comfortable retirement.

The critical aspect of this strategy is understanding the rules and restrictions. You also need to take time to find the right lender who'd be willing to work with you and offer decent conditions.

When I say decent conditions, I mean a deposit of around 20% and an interest rate that makes sense from an investment perspective.

Assuming you get all that right, the only challenge is finding the property that has the potential to bring in the highest possible returns. But don't worry, I'm here to help you with that.

CHAPTER 16

Mindset and Goal Setting

So far, we have mostly talked about the technical aspects of property investments. However, having the right mindset to take the plunge and purchase your first property is equally important.

With that in mind, it's best to consider the story of one of my clients so you understand exactly what I'm getting at.

This client is actually a family of five that has outgrown their three-bedroom house. Their goal was to get a bigger home, but they also wanted another property they could use to repay their loan quicker.

Knowing all that, we decided that the best strategy was to purchase land and build a dual occupancy. And it wasn't long before the perfect plot appeared on the market in the Hills District, NSW.

The land size was 615sqm, more than enough to build a five-bedroom home and a granny flat in a growth corridor.

Due to the location and development, this was a more expensive deal. However, the family would still get exactly what they wanted, plus amazing rental yields and capital growth.

So, let's talk numbers.

The asking price for the land was $605,000 and we managed to drive that down to $595,000, saving the client $10,000.

The projected building cost for the granny flat was $120,000. But its weekly rental was $400 with annual rental yields of 17%.

At the time of writing, the building plans were still in the DA stage. However, by the time everything is completed, this family will have $1 million+ in property in an area with great capital growth. More importantly, their budget won't be under major strain.

The key thing is that they've set their minds to do it and weren't afraid to take the plunge. And once their goals were in place, it was only a matter of dealing with the technicalities.

Therefore, I want to help you get in the right mindset and set your goals straight.

The Six Mindset Habits That Set You Up for Investing Success

#1 – Outcome-Focused Thinking

With property investments, you can expect challenges from the get-go. But don't get me wrong, I don't mean to scare you or anything.

Knowing how to grapple with the challenges is a critical aspect of your mindset. You shouldn't succumb to the stress of it and keep wondering why something is happening to you.

It's not only you. Every investor faces similar issues.

But the difference between great and average investors is in how they deal with those issues.

Simply put, they focus on the outcomes only. The proper investor mindset is to start thinking about the things you can do to fix a problem as soon as it arises.

If you waste your time whining and feeling blocked, there's no way to move forward.

#2 – Definition of the Outcome

Yes, you need to focus on the outcome, but what is it?

It's safe to say that the desired outcome is a bit different for every investor. Still, there are specific guidelines on how to define an outcome for yourself.

In a nutshell, the idea is to focus on the where, what, and when.

That means you should be specific about the thing you want, when you want it to happen, and what's the timeline to reach your goal.

The critical thing here is not to rush anything and avoid comparing yourself to other property investors. Instead, define the steps that bring you closer to the favourable outcome and work at your own pace without hesitation.

#3 – The Dynamics of a Deal

It would be wrong to expect a deal to go smoothly from start to finish.

Of course, you can do certain things pretty quickly, but expect to encounter tasks that could make you struggle.

And if you are to overcome the struggles and sleep well at night, you need to be flexible. It's important to accept things for what they are. Also, you need to be aware of your dependencies to push the deal through.

It's hard to finalise the whole deal on your own. This is why you need to understand whom to rely on to complete some vital tasks regarding your property investment.

#4 – Business Mindset

Yes, there's a promise of financial freedom with property investments. But it's better to refer to this investor benefit as independence rather than freedom.

Why?

Knowing that you want to achieve independence, it becomes easier to view your investments as a business. More importantly, it helps you run the investments like a business.

And I'm assuming your goal isn't only to purchase a few properties and earn just enough so you don't need to worry about your expenses.

Rather, you want to build a portfolio that will significantly boost your family's finances and leave a lasting legacy for future generations.

#5 – Debt and Liability

Some potential investors get scared by debt, and that may discourage them from investing. But unless you've accumulated a lot of capital, debt is inevitable.

That being said, there are ways to make debt less emotional or stressful.

Start by determining how well your debt is covered. You should have a strategy to keep your family and yourself covered from debt if something goes south.

Taking out an insurance policy for each property in your portfolio is a great way to eliminate some of the risks. But what if something unexpected happens to you?

Again, life insurance is there to help. You should take out a comprehensive policy that protects both your finances and business in case of disability or death.

#6 – Practicing the Mindset

You should always work on your mindset and double your efforts to find the right solution for each problem that may arise.

One of the main challenges is that novice investors struggle to find good deals when they start. But there's a way out.

First, I can help you find the most optimal deal that's in line with your goals. But I want to teach you how to create deals rather than wait for the perfect thing to come up in the market.

Why It's So Important That You Set Goals

Keep in mind that if you don't set your goals, it's tough to know if you're moving in the right direction. Also, you'll struggle to take informed steps in your investor journey, which may lead to making a lot of mistakes.

Now, I'm sure you understand that your 9-to-5 doesn't move the dial and that you need more to secure a comfortable lifestyle.

But have you actually taken the time to devise a strategy that would pull you out of your situation?

Okay, since you're reading this book, you've nailed the critical first step, which is understanding what it is that can provide a better standard of living.

However, that's only the first step. Next, you need to create an action plan, leave all the distractions aside and focus on landing your first property deal.

To that end, you don't want to only set a goal then wait until the conditions are favourable for you to start investing. Instead, you have to be proactive and understand how to work with the resources that you already have.

As mentioned in other chapters, leverage allows you to get in on the game with limited resources. Then, when you build a solid foundation for your portfolio, you can move on to better, more profitable deals. This is exactly how I did it.

Therefore, the first thing to do is figure out your starting point and your goals. When doing so, it pays to be very specific. You want to plot out every detail so you have a better understanding of the steps to get there.

Lastly, it's vital to adopt positive habits from the actions you take and talk to people about what you want to achieve.

By taking the right actions, you're building an investment routine that's much less stressful and helps with your confidence. And talking to other like-minded people makes you more accountable and motivated to push through.

Three Tips for Setting Realistic and Achievable Goals

#1 – Setting the Timeframe and Budget

As mentioned in the previous section, you need to assess your current financial standing. That helps you determine what kind of property you'll be able to afford and if you need to make certain sacrifices.

The given action also helps you safeguard your investment for the long haul, and it buys you peace of mind.

Additionally, you should consider creating a maintenance fund, particularly if you're buying a property to rent out. It would be okay to set aside a fraction of the rental returns every month or two weeks. Down the line, that money should be enough to cover even nightmarish, unexpected repairs.

When it comes to the timeframe, it's important not to rush. Think about how many years you'll be investing.

Some investors want to get out in just five years. But my advice is to stick it out for ten or more years. The lengthy timeframe gives you plenty of options to build a sizeable portfolio and achieve your financial goals.

#2 – Why You're Investing

I bet you're investing to achieve financial freedom and independence and create an asset base that may secure future generations.

That's perfectly fine, but your reasons to invest need to be more specific than that.

We already discussed that you're looking for properties that offer high capital growth. And you should make that the first reason to invest.

The second reason could be securing a passive income from renting out your properties. Sure, this income isn't going to be that high at first. But a few years down the line, it could replace your current income.

Finally, the reason to invest could be tax breaks, but I'd advise you not to focus on that too much. Otherwise, you might be compelled to try your luck with negatively-geared properties that might hurt your future investment capacity.

#3 – *How to Be a Landlord*

Being a landlord requires a bit of work, and you need to be ready to make decisions regarding your tenants, maintenance, rent, leases, etc.

Before you rent a property, it's essential to consider what kind of tenants would work best for you. Also, set a target for the rent price to cover all the costs, maintenance and repairs included. In addition, make sure that there's some money left for you.

To figure out the right price, it's best to talk to the real estate agents that specialise in a particular area. They'll be able to give you a pretty accurate estimate on property management costs, additional fees, and tenant demographics.

Getting the Right Mindset

For some, purchasing the first investment property is a daunting experience. They feel they don't have the sufficient knowledge and expertise to take the first step.

But throughout this book, I've shared the experiences of my clients, most of whom had no prior knowledge of property investments. Regardless, they were super successful with a little bit of professional help.

Why?

The main reason was that they adopted the investor mindset and started making moves believing they're building a legacy business for themselves and their families.

Sure, there are many technical aspects, rules, and regulations to keep in mind. But once you get a handle on those, investing becomes your second nature.

Even so, procrastination is one of the worst enemies for novice investors. And that's why I decided to dedicate the entire next chapter to that.

CHAPTER 17

Procrastination vs Action Taking

Like with all other chapters, I'd like to open with a client story here.

But before that, let me put you in a hypothetical situation.

You've been reading and learning about property investments for quite some time and even started checking out what's available in and around your location.

Then, you began budgeting for the investment and figuring out your current finance to determine how much money you need.

But once you've done all the analysis and assessment, you get a peculiar stage fright. You have everything ready and it's looking good on paper, however, you fail to take the first step.

Now, you're not the only one to feel like that, many investors faced similar challenges. Here, I'd like to give you an example of what happens if you don't let procrastination prevent you from taking the first step.

The client in question is an established cardiologist who had the equity to invest in property.

Even so, the goal was to minimise risk as much as possible. Also, the client wanted to ensure he could leverage other professionals' expertise to further grow his wealth.

Why?

He understood the time was right to invest in property, but he didn't want to waste any time trying to learn all the odds and ends of the business.

Instead, his goal was to continue doing interventional cardio-thoracic medicine while somebody helped him build an outstanding property portfolio.

I know that you may believe that having the equity to invest removed much of the client's procrastination, but it wasn't like that at all.

He understood the potential returns he could be getting from property investments. More importantly, he knew that waiting could make his investment less profitable.

So, we had a sit down to create a strategy that would work best for the client's long-term goals.

We decided to go for a development project where we'd build five townhouses and sell them all. And the perfect property appeared in the South Coast, NSW.

The land size was 1100sqm, and there was an existing house that the client could rent out while waiting to get the development approvals. After the approval, the strategy was to demolish the current house, subdivide the land, and build the five townhouses.

This allowed the client to maximise the land and the returns on investment. Even better, the purchase price for the existing house and land was only $620,000, leaving a substantial budget for the development.

At the time of writing, the project was still underway. But when all is finished and sold, it'll make the client a millionaire.

The True Costs of Procrastination in Property

The thing you need to understand is that if you keep putting off your investment goals, you're likely to pay more. This applies to the actual cost of a house, for example, and the opportunity cost.

To make matters more complicated, if you're prone to procrastination, you may find it hard to break the habit. The main reason is that you might be frozen by analysis paralysis.

Simply, this is a confusing feeling after you've done all the necessary steps before buying the property. But then, you're not sure what to purchase because you can't single out one option as the best.

On top of that, some people tend to self-sabotage because of fear. As mentioned, they think the supposed lack of expertise will lead them to make a terrible mistake.

However, this couldn't be further from the truth.

The reality is that it's better to try something and fail than do nothing at all. Plus, you shouldn't forget that all the help you need is at your fingertips. So, there's little room for making mistakes.

More importantly, missing your chance to invest may result in you losing the opportunistic window to get the best deal. But this merits more explanation.

How Many Lilies Are in Your Pond

To explain the window of opportunity and how much it could affect the cost of investment, I'd like to use an analogy involving lilies.

Think about the property market as a relatively big pond where you plant the lilies. For the sake of argument, we'll say that the number of lilies doubles every month.

Like properties, the lilies in this analogy have the power to compound as time goes by. But let me dive into that a bit further.

So, you plant one lily (think of it as your first property) and, the following month, you have two. Then, the month after that, you have four, and the lilies keep doubling as time goes by.

Now, let's say it takes about four years for the lilies to cover about 15% of the pond. The month after that, 30% of the pond will get covered.

Sure, in property investments, time is usually measured in years instead of months. But your portfolio can compound the same way the lilies in the analogy do.

The first year, you get only one, then the second year, you get another property. However, from the third year on, you may keep doubling your portfolio based on the existing returns from your properties and capital growth.

And what happens if you choose to wait for another year before investing?

Chances are you've significantly shrunk your opportunistic window and cut the compounding effect in half. Plus, you'll need to pay more because planting lilies becomes more expensive each year.

Of course, this is just an analogy to show you how much you're missing out on if you procrastinate. But you also need to keep in mind that you have a limited time window to make investments.

This is the number of years you can devote to building your portfolio. And your goals and readiness are much different when you're 30 compared to when you're 50.

Yes, it's possible to build a portfolio in ten years. But there's still no reason to wait because I'm sure you'll get the bug for property investments and want to do it for more than ten years.

Overcoming Your Fear to Take Action

#1– Decision-making

Decidophobia, which is the decision-making fear, could be one of the reasons you tend to procrastinate. With some people, it may be blown out of proportion so much that they suffer a panic attack every time they're supposed to make a decision.

The more common form of this phobia is a general confusion about decision-making and a lack of motivation to do something. Consequently, this leads to unnatural dependence on other people.

But how do you overcome that?

The tactic is surprisingly simple. You just need to make a lot of decisions daily. These don't need to be anything significant, at first.

Then, when it's time to decide on something that can truly change your life for the better, it'll become easier to take action.

#2 – Starting Small

I know that you have your eyes set on a ten-property portfolio that yields excellent passive income. And I'm sure that you wish to make the first property count as it may set the pace for the rest of your investments.

But you need to be realistic about your purchasing power and property management capacity.

In other words, there's nothing wrong about starting with just a tiny granny flat that offers excellent rental yields and capital gains. Then, it will become much easier for you to avoid procrastination when it's time to buy your next property.

#3 – When to Take Action

I'd say now is the time to take action because your opportunistic window will remain open for a limited time.

Don't take this the wrong way. I'm not suggesting you should jump at the first property that comes your way. Since you're an investor now, it's equally important to know when to move onto the next deal.

What I mean is that some deals may appear very good on paper. But when you scratch the surface, you realise that deal isn't right.

Even so, this doesn't mean you should get discouraged and postpone investing even further. Instead, dive right into assessing the next property that appears promising. Soon enough, you'll find the deal that fits the bill.

#4 – *Staying Informed*

The correct information is worth its weight in gold. Better yet, it helps you build confidence in your decision-making skills.

You should do your best to tune into any available information channel. In particular, it pays to join property investment groups on social media and offline.

Also, make sure to get the latest, most relevant information from industry blogs and podcasts. And get to know real estate agents and other professionals who may provide vital information about the properties you're targeting.

But keep in mind that you need to be very strict when choosing your sources of information. Your goal is to find the experts who have the most experience and the ability to provide concise actionable tips.

#5 – *Learning from Mistakes and Motivation*

You shouldn't waste time feeling sorry for the mistakes you've made. Just analyse your wrongdoings without blaming yourself and create a strategy not to repeat the same thing.

By doing that, you're creating a framework to grow and learn throughout your investor journey. And you'll also be boosting your confidence and motivation to keep landing the most profitable deals.

Turning Procrastination into Action – The Five Tips

#1 – Start Now

I've stressed this a few times, and I'll do it again. There's no point in waiting to begin your journey as a real estate investor.

Why?

For one, the longer you wait, the more you close your opportunistic window to land excellent property deals. And you're likely to pay more since the increases in the property prices aren't going to slow down.

Then, procrastination puts you at risk of analysis paralysis. Of course, assessing each property and learning about the industry is essential. But you need to draw the line somewhere and trust your judgement to make the right call.

#2 – Importance of Focus

In property investments, the focus is all about having a great strategy and sticking to it.

You should have an actionable plan about what type of real estate to focus on. And the same goes for the location and critical elements of a property that make it lucrative.

Now, I understand that venturing out a little bit can be profitable. But at the beginning of your investor journey, you need laser focus to nail the first deal. Diversifying does more harm than good here.

#3 – The Five-Minute Miracle

The *Five-Minute Miracle* is a technique that could help you overcome procrastination. And practising this technique is straightforward.

Every day, you should ask yourself the following question:

What is the action to take in under five minutes that helps me move the dial a little bit?

When you identify that tiny action that pushes you forward a little, set a timer and work on it for five minutes. If you fail to complete the action, that's okay. You can go back to it the next day or extend the time.

The point is that since you've started something, you're more likely to finish it because of personal accountability.

#4 – Kindness

How does kindness help with procrastination?

You need to be kind to yourself and forgive everything you might have missed because of procrastinating. That helps you get in the mindset where you don't judge yourself hence lose motivation to take more actions.

Additionally, being kind helps you work past the procrastination that's plaguing your success right now.

#5 – Understand the Why

The *Why* here refers to the reasons you're procrastinating. We've already discussed that fear could be one of the main culprits. And the best way to overcome fear is to take action.

But if it's not fear, you need to think carefully about the reasons that prevent you from doing what's right.

Okay, some of you may argue that you don't have enough time to dedicate to real estate. Now, I want you to remember the clients mentioned in the previous chapters.

Most of them were working professionals, so not having the time is just an excuse to procrastinate.

Don't Procrastinate

Procrastination is among the worst enemies of novice investors.

There are so many people who've done all the pre-investing work and got fantastic knowledge. But when it was time to take the plunge, they got cold feet.

I'm sure that you don't want to be one of those people because this penultimate chapter gave you more than enough tips to kill your procrastination.

CHAPTER 18

Your Future and Where You're Now

As mentioned in the first chapter, I've come a long way since arriving in Australia.

With only $50 to my name and a family to support, I succeeded in building the life for myself that I dreamed about.

Like you, I was a working professional with very little time to dedicate to anything else. However, I never stopped learning and was brave enough to venture into properties knowing I was building my legacy.

But why am I telling you all this?

The point is that I'm not special or didn't have some exceptional education that made me a successful investor.

No, I did it all through hard work, learning, and perseverance. And yes, I made some mistakes and purchased properties that I shouldn't have.

However, that didn't discourage me from going forward. Instead, I carefully considered what went wrong and devised a winning strategy that led me to amazing success.

Now, I'm sure the road won't be so bumpy for you!

I made it my mission to share all the knowledge and help others reach their dreams of financial freedom and independence.

In this last chapter, I'd like to touch upon some of the key points discussed in the book.

Why Is Property a Good Choice?

First of all, studies show that property is one of the most stable asset classes in terms of capital growth. And it has been like that for decades.

Okay, you can expect some turbulence. But it's not like you're going to lose all your money investing in properties, as long as you do it wisely. As a quick reminder, I'd like to reiterate the four key benefits of property investments:

1. Amazing ROI (Return on Investment)
2. Tax benefits
3. Plenty of financing options
4. Security

These benefits show that you don't need a lot of cash to get in on the game. You just need enough to cover the down payment on your first property and use leverage to grow your portfolio.

Sure, the COVID situation might have slowed things a little bit. But this is actually a chance for you because the interest rates will remain low. Better yet, the demand for residential properties is soon going to reach an all-time high.

Getting Into Your Investor Journey

By now, you should feel motivated and anxious to purchase your first property.

That's great, but remember that the journey has distinct stages where you need to act accordingly:

1. Accumulation – this is where you build the foundation for your portfolio and passive income. For that reason, you need to focus only on A-grade properties.
2. Consolidation – in this stage, you'll be reducing your lifestyle cost to further boost your cash flow and grow the portfolio. Plus, you'd be looking for ways to speed up the payments on your properties.

3. Legacy – during the legacy stage, you get to reap the benefits of all your hard work. This is when you can cash out or continue living the dream through all the passive income you acquired. Even so, many investors choose to continue because property got into their blood.

Negative Gearing Revisited

Throughout the book, I kept stressing that negative gearing is dangerous for your portfolio and profit. And this is particularly true for novice investors.

I understand that it could sound enticing because of the tax benefits and the relatively low price of negatively-geared properties. But these usually turn into a significant money pit where you'll need to finance something out of pocket just to keep the investment.

Even worse, negative gearing might push you to sell the property off at a loss to avoid putting your family under a lot of financial strain.

Instead of focusing on negatively-geared properties, you should turn your attention to creative investment strategies. And since there are so many different options, you'll surely find an innovative approach that yields the most profit without burning a hole in your pocket.

The creative strategies you should focus on include renovations, splitter blocks, infill sites, and subdivisions. Venturing into commercial properties is also a perfect creative strategy, but it's usually not for novice investors.

But don't worry, I'm here to help you find just the right strategy that fits your investment goals and budget.

Ideally, you'll be able to find a residential property on a large piece of land. That should allow you to subdivide and rent out the existing house and sell or develop the remaining plot.

The main benefit of this creative strategy is that it maximises the returns on your investment. And this is a good strategy even though it may require a bit more money upfront.

The Retirement of Your Dreams

Once you find the strategy that works best for you, you can repeat it to build the portfolio and benefit from the compounding effect.

The idea is that each property pays for another one through rental yield and capital growth. After a few years, you'll accumulate enough to reduce your portfolio debt and start enjoying passive income.

But why stop at that?

Property investments have the power to secure you a comfortable retirement where you won't need to worry about finance. Once your portfolio is stable and debt-free, keep finding ways to grow it even further to leave a lasting legacy for the generations to come.

Get Into the Investor Mindset

I'm sure this book helped you start thinking like a property investor.

But remember that procrastination and fear are your worst enemies!

However, you have all the power to overcome them and build fantastic wealth. More importantly, you're not in it alone.

Don't hesitate to solicit expert help to reach your goals. You know, you're an investor now and you're not supposed to do all the work on your own.

Rather, perceive the investment journey as if it were a business where you're the boss.

Putting yourself in that frame of mind boosts your decision-making skills, confidence, and success.

So, don't think twice about reaching out to me to assist you in getting your first investment property. That's where your path to wealth begins.

If you want help to kick start your property investments, and change your financial future we are here to help. You can get in touch through the Msisa Property website:

https://msisaproperty.com.au/book-an-appointment/

www.ingramcontent.com/pod-product-compliance
Lightning Source LLC
Chambersburg PA
CBHW072008290426
44109CB00018B/2174